THE TRUTH DETECTOR

ALSO BY JACK SCHAFER, Ph.D., with MARVIN KARLINS, Ph.D.

The Like Switch

THE TRUTH DETECTOR

AN EX-FBI AGENT'S GUIDE
FOR GETTING PEOPLE
TO REVEAL THE TRUTH

JACK SCHAFER, Ph.D.,
with MARVIN KARLINS, Ph.D.

ATRIA PAPERBACK
New York   London   Toronto   Sydney   New Delhi

To my wife, Helen:
For better, for worse, for richer, for
poorer, in sickness and in health,
to love and to cherish, till death do us part.

JACK SCHAFER

To all the men and women who risk their
lives daily to keep America safe:
Your selfless acts of heroism are the gold
standard of human greatness.

MARVIN KARLINS

CONTENTS

SECTION III:

PUTTING YOURSELF TO THE TEST

SECTION I

ELICITATION:
What It Is, How It Works, Why It Works

Getting to the Truth Before the Lie

*If people listened to themselves more
often, they would talk a lot less.*

EDWARD A. MURPHY, JR.

Imagine going up to a stranger in a shopping mall, initiating a conversation, and within five minutes getting them to reveal personal information, such as their Social Security number, computer password, date of birth, or mother's maiden name, without them knowing they provided sensitive personal information. This may seem like an impossible task, but it's easier than you think. I remain astonished at how easy it is to get people to unwittingly provide sensitive information and reveal the truth.

There are dozens of books on detecting deception. This isn't one of them. What makes this book unique is the presentation of a technique you can use to extract honest information from friends, family members, coworkers—even total strangers— without them realizing what you are doing. Using this technique, you can get people to tell you the truth about subjects they would normally keep secret or lie about. That is why the book is called *The Truth Detector* rather than *The Lie Detector*: because once you learn the methods in this book, you will be able to get people to reveal the truth before they ever get suspicious, raise their "shields," and respond deceptively. You can then use that information in a way that will bring you the greatest possible benefit. Knowing what people really think can even help you distinguish a friend from a potential enemy who can do you harm. Because this approach was designed to elicit a truthful response from people, the technique is referred to as *elicitation*.

As an FBI special agent, my job was to obtain information from suspects, witnesses, and spies who, for various reasons, wanted to keep that information private. Elicitation is an essential, noninvasive tool that I helped develop over my career in the intelligence field to collect information. Because of my years of experience as a member of the FBI's National Security Division Behavioral Analysis Program, I was often called upon to teach young FBI trainees how to use the elicitation techniques to obtain maximum results. These intelligence officers, in the course of their work, are often required to obtain information that is not publicly available.

To demonstrate the power and effectiveness of the elicitation technique, I conducted a classroom demonstration. I confidently assured my students that, at the end of the eight-hour elicitation training course, they would be able to obtain dates of birth, PIN numbers, Social Security numbers, bank account information, and computer passwords from perfect strangers within a few minutes of meeting them.

Naturally, the students were very skeptical of my claim. They assured me that no one would give up sensitive, personal information to a stranger, much less not realize they were revealing that critical information. It was clear to me that they believed my claims were not only beyond absurd but tested the limits of human imagination. One defiant student vehemently proclaimed that he would *never* give personal information to a stranger under *any* circumstances.

In the first four hours of the training session, I taught the students basic elicitation techniques, the exact ones you will be learning about in this book. During this time, I kept in mind what the defiant student had insisted. My goal was to get this individual to reveal his Social Security number without him realizing he had done so.

I knew the topic of eliciting Social Security numbers would come up naturally during class discussions. When it did, I explained the components of a Social Security number. I began the discussion with the last four digits on the Social Security card. I told the students that these four digits alone were not very important, because more than one person can be assigned the same four digits. In fact, out of 10,000 people, at least two people will share the same last four digits of their Social Security numbers. I also reminded the students that those last four digits of their Social Security numbers were useless if the other five numbers were unknown.

At this point, I turned to the defiant student and said, "Knowing this, you wouldn't object to revealing the last four numbers of your Social Security number, would you?" The student shrugged his shoulders and recited the four digits.

Next, I casually mentioned that the middle two digits were "group numbers" and virtually meaningless because they simply reflected the order in which the total Social Security number was assigned to new applicants. I asked a student if she would object to revealing the middle two digits of her Social Security number. She blurted out two numbers. I pointed to another student and, without saying a word, he recited the two digits of his own Social Security number. In quick succession, I pointed to random students. They automatically recited the two middle digits of their Social Security numbers without hesitation. I then pointed to the defiant student; he blurted out his Social Security number's two middle digits as well. To camouflage my elicitation objective, I pointed to several more students, who willingly gave their two digits.

I concluded this portion of my lecture by telling the students that the first three digits of a Social Security number corresponded to the location of the Social Security office that issued the number. During one of the morning class breaks, I nonchalantly asked the defiant student where he was from. He readily identified the city and state where he grew up. I surmised that his parents obtained a Social Security number for him in order to write him off as a dependent on their tax returns. I looked up the Social Security office closest to the city where the defiant student grew up and obtained the first three numbers of the student's Social Security number.

At the end of the four-hour block of training, we had lunch and then returned to the classroom, where I prepared the students for the second portion of the training exercise. I explained that they were to go to a nearby shopping mall and spend the afternoon eliciting personal information from random strangers.

Prior to dismissing the students, I walked up to the whiteboard. With a dry-erase pen I wrote in big numbers the Social Security number of the defiant student. I turned and looked at him. His eyes were fixed on the number and his jaw was slack. After a few seconds the shock wore off and he blurted out, "That's not fair. You cheated!" I reminded him that fair play doesn't count when it comes to espionage, a world he was about to enter. I sternly warned the rest of the students that even the most security-conscious people can become victims of elicitation, a lesson the defiant student will remember the rest of his life.

After several hours of practice in the shopping mall, the students were amazed at how many people revealed sensitive information without realizing it. The part that intrigued the students most was that they could accomplish this amazing feat after only four hours of classroom instruction.

So can you. Once you learn how to use the elicitation techniques in this book, you will have taken your first important step toward achieving this objective. I have purposely included actual examples of elicitation from the everyday kinds of situations you will find yourself in. As you read these examples to learn how elicitation is used, you will also discover how to apply this knowledge in a variety of social and business settings.

Simply summarized: By effectively utilizing elicitation, you will be in a better position to gain a greater amount of *true* information that might otherwise be lost and, at the same time, enhance your interpersonal effectiveness with others, whether they be strangers, casual acquaintances, or those closest to you.

Elicitation is the master key in truth detection, but like all interviewing techniques, its value is maximized when certain conditions are met. Creating those conditions involves understanding and utilizing the factors that underpin the successful elicitation process—factors that you can use to enhance the power of elicitation in obtaining the truth you seek. Once you've familiarized yourself with them, you'll be ready to make yourself a successful truth detector.

Let's get started!

CHAPTER 1

So Much for Shredders

All truths are easy to understand once they are
discovered; the point is to discover them.
GALILEO GALILEI

The desire to know if someone is lying or telling the truth is as old as Adam and Eve in the Garden of Eden. And why not? How we act, how successful we are—even our survival—can be profoundly impacted by our ability to determine if information is true or false.

During my two decades as a special agent for the FBI, my job was to assess whether suspects, witnesses, and spies were withholding critical information and/or telling lies that could have far-reaching implications for the safety of specific individuals and, in some cases, the security of the entire country.

The question became: What was the best way to get truthful information from persons of interest? The traditional approach involved attempting to determine if the person was lying in the first place. This involved using mechanical devices (polygraph machines), physical observation (watching for nonverbal cues of deception), and various forms of interrogation designed to get the targeted individual to admit his or her dishonesty. But there was a problem with this approach: Even if it was successful in determining a person's veracity, it came at a high cost. When people become aware that their honesty is being challenged, their "shields" go up, and whenever that happens, they are unlikely to voluntarily reveal the information they know. In fact, the opposite occurs: these individuals "clam up," "lawyer up," or "dummy up," making any attempt to get information out of them a daunting if not impossible task. Thus, what happened when the traditional approach was used was that investigators could sometimes tell if certain information was true but lost the chance to discover other information that might have been even more valuable.

This made me and a group of my colleagues wonder if there was a better way to get people to reveal true information *before* they went into lying mode. I suspected that if individuals were not aware that I was trying to get critical information from them, they would be more likely to reveal it. Only if they became cognizant of my intentions would they become defensive, raise their shields, and begin withholding information and telling lies. Our strategy, then, was to get to the truth before the lies—in other words, extract the relevant information from a person of interest without them becoming aware of our intentions. If this could be achieved, the credibility of the information would almost always be solid and we could obtain it without the person shifting into information-withholding, lie-generating mode.

ELICITATION: LEARN THE TRUTH BEFORE THE LIE

Noting the flaws in the traditional interrogation techniques, I worked with my colleagues to come up with less confrontational techniques based on psychology and natural human behaviors as opposed to the more confrontational, old-school law enforcement interviewing techniques currently being used. The result was the noninvasive approach of elicitation—so named because it was designed to elicit the truth rather than detect lies. Elicitation techniques are relatively easy to master, because it is based on normal behaviors people rely on during conversations. Over my career I developed several elicitation techniques designed to extract information. These involve a conversational style whereby you use words in a way that encourages people to reveal the truth without them becoming aware of what you are attempting to accomplish. I will be teaching you these techniques in the coming chapters, but first I think it may help you understand elicitation more clearly if I present you with some historical perspective on how the technique was developed.

CREATING THE RIGHT ENVIRONMENT FOR ELICITATION

Possibly the most famous pioneer in using elicitation-style strategy was Hanns-Joachim Scharff (1907–1992). He worked for the German Luftwaffe at the intelligence and evaluation center in Oberursel, Germany, and became one of the most successful interrogators during World War II.

Scharff's interrogation techniques deviated from those used by the feared German Gestapo. The Gestapo used emotional pain, physical deprivation, and authority in attempting to gain intelligence. Conversely, Scharff was noted for his friendly, conversational interrogation approach. He created a nonthreatening, noninvasive, comfortable environment wherein he rarely asked specific questions. In almost all cases Scharff would take his targets for a walk around the airfield with no guards nearby and engage them in what they thought was a casual conversation. His technique became known as the "change-of-scene" approach: giving his prisoner the impression that they were safe speaking to him. Since they then believed that this was *not* an interrogation, they felt more comfortable talking and telling the truth. Scharff wanted them to regard the interrogation room as the only place that an interrogation took place. He also created the illusion that he knew more information than he did. He would present information and then simply wait for the prisoner to either confirm or deny his statement.

After the war ended and the prisoners were repatriated, one of them commented, "You would impulsively pop off and correct him [Scharff]—probably this was one of his tactics.* Prisoners were more willing to confirm information they believed was already known for several reasons. First, they wanted to give the impression of minimal cooperation to avoid harsher interrogation techniques. Second, prisoners rationalized that no harm could be done if they merely corroborated information the enemy already knew as opposed to providing previously unknown information.

Scharff often told long, detailed stories, giving the prisoners the impression that he knew all, when in fact he knew very

---

*Quoted in R. F. Toliver, *The Interrogator: The Story of Hanns Joachim Scharff, Master Interrogator of the Luftwaffe* (Atglen, PA: Schiffer Publishing), p. 138.

little. In the process of confirming information, prisoners often provided new details. To confuse the prisoners even further, Scharff's conversational technique camouflaged the objectives of his interrogation. Scharff did not press prisoners for information but rather created a conversational environment wherein they were inclined to speak freely. When prisoners provided new information, Scharff would act as if he already knew what they were talking about and that the information was of little importance. As Scharff's interrogations continued, it became clear over time that the information prisoners provided in response to his friendly approach was more likely to be truthful. They were not trained to resist Scharff's congenial interrogation techniques and revealed critical intelligence information without realizing they were supplying details they would not have revealed under harsher interrogation techniques.

On one occasion Scharff was tasked with finding out why American fighter aircraft machine guns fired tracer bullets of a certain color. During a conversation with an American pilot held in a prisoner-of-war camp, Scharff casually brought up the subject. He made a presumptive statement (a form of elicitation; See Chapter 4), giving the pilot the illusion that he already knew the reason for the different-colored tracers. Unwittingly, the pilot revealed the true purpose of the bullets, which was simple: The different color was used to let pilots know when their ammunition was running low. The Germans were much relieved to obtain this information, because they had believed the tracers were being used for a far more sinister purpose.

Scharff was successful in extracting true information from prisoners of war because he understood the importance of *empathy* and *rapport*, two essential qualities to harness in order to effectively use elicitation. He imagined himself in the place of the prisoner, believing he would be more likely to communicate with his interrogator if he were treated with respect. Scharff also suspected prisoners would be more likely to reveal information if they liked their interrogator, so he tried to cultivate a rapport with those he interrogated.

Scharff's insights were important, conceptual contributions to the enhanced elicitation approach you will be learning in this book. I will return to them in the next chapter. But first, let me give you another example of how the elicitation process works, using a gadget some automobile drivers are unaware is hidden within arm's length of their steering wheel.

ASK A PERSON OR "TELL A MATIC"?

Pretend for a moment that you're trying to get the very best auto insurance rate for your newly purchased car. You are an aggressive driver who has a lead foot and doesn't mind taking a few risks on the road.

Your agent asks, "Are you a safe driver?"

What answer do you provide?

Or suppose you are in a hurry to get home one night and are driving recklessly, speeding to reach your destination. A few blocks short of your house, you run a red light and collide with another vehicle. There are no witnesses to the accident except you and the other driver. The police arrive and an officer pulls you aside and asks if you were driving safely. What answer do you give?

In both of the above examples, you might reply truthfully and admit to being an unsafe driver, but many people aren't so honest. Faced with getting something they want (lower insurance rates) and something they don't want (a traffic ticket, or legal liability), it's more likely they would be less than forthcoming. It's so much easier to say "I'm a safe driver" than tell the truth and suffer the consequences.

Enter "telematics." Over the last several years, auto insurance companies have been promoting tracking devices, known in the industry as "telematic devices," to follow the driving habits of their customers.* These cigarette pack–size devices, which fit under the dashboard of your car, can track any number of your driving habits, such as speed, braking, acceleration, distance traveled, time of usage, number of collision and lane-change warnings—even where you are located. (Lots of stops at liquor stores are not recommended!)

Obviously, when it comes to determining the truth of how someone drives, it's better to check out what a tracker has to say than to ask the driver directly. The same holds true for elicitation. Properly done, you will be able to get more useful information from people and have greater confidence that what they say is true if they don't suspect you are purposely pumping them for information or challenging their honesty.

BE A TRUTH TRACKER: ELICITATION IS YOUR GPS

A person who effectively uses elicitation to obtain true information should basically operate like an automobile tracking device. The information received should be accurate and provide the specific details needed to achieve the elicitor's objective. Further, the person giving the information should be unaware that their

---

*J. Vincent and C. Threewitt, "How Do Those Car Insurance Tracking Devices Work?" *U.S. News & World Report*, February 26, 2018.

responses are being purposely solicited to benefit the elicitor in any form or manner, just as a driver would be unaware if someone secretly put a tracking device in their car. Fortunately, because of human nature and the conversational approach utilized, effective elicitation, with reasonable practice and use, is relatively easy to achieve. I know that's true because I've taught people from all walks of life and educational backgrounds to use elicitation successfully.

Elicitation techniques work because they're based on scientific knowledge of how people behave. Elicitors take advantage of these basic human behaviors to obtain the information they seek. They understand that specific conversational approaches work best in predisposing people to talk freely and divulge truths they would not otherwise reveal if they felt someone was "digging" for information.

A properly conducted elicitation session is a positive experience. Unlike interrogation, the person being elicited will not experience physical or mental discomfort; in fact, they will feel good about themselves, because the elicitor makes them the focus of the conversation. The fact is most people *like* to be the focus of attention. Elicitors use this natural human trait to their advantage. They also use empathy and other rapport-building techniques, discussed in the next chapter, to build a positive relationship with a person of interest. The more comfortable the elicitation target is with the elicitor, the more information that individual is likely to divulge.

Elicitation targets will not be anxious or suspicious during your conversations with them because the focus of the conversation will be all about them. Most people are comfortable talking about themselves. It is rare in today's world to find someone willing to really listen to another individual's concerns, their professional frustrations, and their solutions for their own (or the world's) problems. People feel comfortable with someone who listens to them and responds empathetically to their ideas and opinions. If *you* are that kind of caring person who is able to listen and put yourself in the other person's shoes while at the same time focusing on them instead of yourself, then you will be an excellent elicitor in a great position to obtain the information you seek.

Since elicitation techniques are designed to keep persons of interest from realizing they are the targets of this information-gathering approach, it's essential not to raise "red flags" that might make a subject aware of the elicitor's intentions. As humans, we often act instinctively without thinking about what we are doing or saying. I sometimes experience this phenomenon when I'm driving a familiar route, like going home from the office for more than the thousandth time. I will drive from work to my house and not have any recollection of how I got there or what happened along the way. This is because my driving pattern has become so deeply ingrained that it allows my brain to go on "autopilot" and get me to my destination without conscious effort. However, if something out of the ordinary occurs during my drive, my brain jolts me into conscious awareness, preparing me to deal with a potentially dangerous situation.

This automatic behavior occurs during the elicitation process as well. Our brains often perform routine interpersonal tasks without our conscious awareness. We spend much of our day on autopilot, allowing us to think about other things or simply daydream. Elicitation techniques are designed to emulate naturally occurring human activities that cause our brains to automatically respond to elicitation prompts without thinking: just as when we find ourselves driving "automatically," we are not fully aware of what we are doing or saying. In this state, unless something is said or done to arouse a person from their "cognitive cruise control," they will be unaware that they are revealing sensitive, personal information.

One of the greatest benefits of employing elicitation, when properly executed, is that the elicitation target will like you. Elicitation is not adversarial or confrontational in nature. It is the opposite. It is best utilized during normal friendly conversations. People talk to people they like, and they do not talk to people they do not like. In the next chapter I will show the elicitation process and how you can quickly establish rapport with people you are approaching for the first time (or do not know very well) or reinforce good rapport with people you are already on familiar terms with. Establishing immediate rapport, especially when meeting a stranger, is a critical element in elicitation—and more important, if achieved, the targeted individual(s) will look forward to meeting with you in the future to unknowingly provide you with additional sensitive, proprietary, and even highly confidential information.

It is important to remember that elicitation works best when the elicitor succeeds in making his or her target feel good about themselves. This is a win-win situation: you obtain the truthful information you are seeking, and the targeted individual walks away feeling good about themselves—and you—at the end of the conversation.

ELICITATION: THE TRUTH TOOL AT YOUR DISPOSAL

Information is the lifeblood of human communication. People want to know what other people are thinking and feeling. For obvious reasons people opt to keep personal information private to avoid identity theft and other inappropriate use. Individuals also avoid sharing their true feelings, especially in today's politically charged environment, to avoid awkward or potentially embarrassing social situations. People in business intentionally withhold information to gain an advantage over a competitor or to enhance their positions during negotiations. Teens often dodge parental inquiries regarding their social lives and personal habits. In some circumstances people withhold information from their significant others.

Knowing how to elicit what people are *truthfully* thinking and feeling will enhance your relationships with them, whether your relationship is social or business related. This is because you will be in a far better position to solve problems when you know what a person truly believes. It allows you to reach decisions in a manner that they can walk away from feeling that a fair deal has been struck, or a decision has been reached that everyone can live with.

Elicitation skills can also help parents create better relationships with their children, especially teens, who are so often reluctant to discuss their true thoughts, feelings, and activities with Mom and Dad. Elicitation techniques, when properly used, create an environment where children *want* to talk to their parents. This in turn affords the parents more time to teach and advise their children on how to cope with their current circumstances as well as the challenges they will face as adults.

Personal relationships can also benefit from the application of elicitation techniques. In numerous relationships, particularly newer ones, people are reluctant to reveal too much about themselves to avoid embarrassment or because they are just naturally reserved. The more personal information that people share with one another, the closer their relationships become. Creating intimacy through the appropriate use of elicitation increases the possibility of meaningful conversations, strengthening social bonds.

Businesspeople can employ elicitation to gain a critical advantage in an increasingly competitive work world. In today's global economy, where the only constant is change, more and more businesses are discovering the importance of collecting information about their competitors as well as the necessity of protecting proprietary information. Making the correct business decisions can mean the difference between prosperity and bankruptcy. This book will equip you with the elicitation tools and techniques to help you gather true information that gives your company or organization a competitive edge without having to hire and depend on expensive, outsourced business intelligence consultants.

SETTING OFF ON YOUR VOYAGE TO VERACITY

You too can become a truth detector once you have learned and become proficient at using the various elicitation approaches described in this book. Being successful involves a degree of commitment on your part. Good elicitation, like any skill, requires a certain amount of practice and regular use to be truly effective. But you *can* achieve these skills. I have taught people from all walks of life—people just like you—to successfully employ these techniques. And be assured you will be richly rewarded for your efforts. Getting people to tell you the truth before they shift into lying mode will give you a decided advantage in your dealings with them.

To get the most out of the following chapters, pay attention to the various elicitation techniques and employ the ones you feel most comfortable using. The more techniques you can use, the better you will be at getting people to tell you the truth. Each technique comes with true, real-world examples that will help you learn the approach while giving you an appreciation for the kinds of information people are willing to reveal when elicitation is used.

Learning about elicitation will also help you avoid becoming a target of the technique and giving up information yourself. You will learn a strategy for recognizing elicitation when it is being used on you, how to fend off these efforts, and, at the same time, maintain a cordial relationship with the person trying to get you to reveal information. Such knowledge is important. Examples will be given to show how elicitation, unrecognized and in the wrong hands, can be used to commit corporate espionage.

Finally, at the end of the book, you will be given two self-administered tests to help you assess your understanding of the material presented in the book. I have no doubt you will pass with flying colors!

The Truth Detector is your guidebook to a deeper understanding of what people really think and what they know. It is a map to help you interpret their behavior correctly. As author Barry Long once observed, "Truth cannot be taught but it is quickly recognized by the person ready to discover it." The journey to that discovery starts now.

CHAPTER 2

Building Rapport: The Foundation of Elicitation

When you lose your ego, you win. It really is that simple.

SHANNON L. ALDER

Whether you are an avid gardener who wants to create the perfect flower bed or a commercial farmer looking to get the highest crop yield, one factor remains the same: Proper preparation for planting is necessary to get maximum desired results. That might involve adding nutrients to the soil, choosing the right kind of bulb or seed for the climate and geography where it will be grown, and choosing the right time, temperature, soil moisture, and soil density for planting . . . all to achieve "green thumb" status when your efforts bear fruit (or roses or corn).

The same is true for anyone who wants to become an effective elicitor. You can simply skip over this chapter, learn the various elicitation techniques that follow, and use them to seek the truth from persons of interest. And it might work, just like I could randomly plant some vegetable seeds in my yard and end up with a bumper crop of carrots and tomatoes. But the odds of being successful in the endeavor drop significantly. If you really want to harvest truth most effectively, you will need to "prep the soil," so to speak. Specifically, you will want to establish rapport with a person of interest if you want to maximize your chances of getting the veracity you desire. In this chapter I will be discussing rapport and ways to establish it.

HARVESTING THE TRUTH . . . AND MORE

Again, the main reason to learn about and establish rapport is that, used in conjunction with the elicitation techniques beginning in Chapter 5, it greatly enhances your chances of getting people to tell you the truth. But there is another reason to learn about and establish rapport: it builds better interpersonal relationships and ways to establish it. This is a collateral benefit that will serve you well even if you *never* use it to elicit the truth.

The relationship between rapport building and positive interpersonal relationships is discussed in greater length and depth in our book *The Like Switch: An Ex–FBI Agent's Guide to Influencing, Attracting, and Winning People Over* but will be abbreviated here to give you just what you need to know to behave appropriately before and during an elicitation session to maximize your chances for a truthful encounter. Once you develop your rapport-building skills, they will become second nature and you will find yourself using them automatically, much as I was able to drive home from work without really thinking about what I was doing.

WHAT IS RAPPORT?

Rapport can be envisioned as a bridge that links two or more people in a positive manner. When you want to elicit something from a person of interest, building rapport with that individual is helpful in making them more willing to share information with you. To establish rapport, there are a few surefire ways to encourage that person to like you. Obviously, how easy it is to accomplish this objective depends on how well you know the person and any history you share with them. If the person you want to elicit information from is a stranger, like a salesperson you approach to buy a product, then the rapport-building process is rather quick and simple. On the other hand, if you are seeking information from someone who already knows you or sees you as a potential threat, the rapport building will be more challenging . . . but not impossible.

Recall the Nazi interrogator Dr. Scharff? The American prisoners certainly didn't count him among their friends; yet, he used certain rapport-building techniques to overcome the prisoners' mistrust of him and get the information he sought. Likewise, I was able to use rapport to draw truthful responses out of criminals who were aware that my purpose was to get them to admit to crimes and send them to prison.

So, how does rapport building work? The three behavioral approaches, which will be highlighted below, have universal applicability and should be used by anyone who wants to maximize their elicitation effectiveness.

APPROACH 1: THE "BIG THREE" NONVERBAL FRIEND SIGNALS

People normally see you before they hear you. Therefore it is important to establish the right mindset in a person of interest before any words are exchanged. Hardwired into our brains is the ability to "scan" approaching individuals and determine from their nonverbal behavior if they are friend or foe. This behavior is automatic. Our brains are continually scanning the environment for friend-or-foe signals. People who give off foe signals are perceived as a threat to be avoided. People who transmit friend signals are viewed as nonthreatening and approachable. When you meet people, especially for the first time, it is critical you send out the right nonverbal cues that allow others to see you in a positive rather than a neutral or negative light.

What exactly are these nonverbal friend signals you can use to enhance your chances of other people taking positive notice of you and lay the positive groundwork for a successful elicitation? There are numerous signals to choose from, but, for our purposes, three critical cues are essential to use if you want others to see you as a friendly person. They are the *eyebrow flash*, the *head tilt*, and the *sincere* (as opposed to fake) *smile*. (Yes, the human brain can detect the difference!)

The Eyebrow Flash

The eyebrow flash is a quick up-and-down movement of the eyebrows that lasts for about one-sixth of a second and is used as a primary, nonverbal friend signal. As you approach another individual, you use the eyebrow flash to send the message that you don't pose a threat. Within five to six feet of meeting someone, our brains look for this signal. If the signal is detected, our nonverbal communication tells the other person we are not an adversary. Most people don't realize that they display an eyebrow flash because the gesture is almost an unconscious one. Most people go through their entire lives without realizing that they use this nonverbal display on a regular basis.

An example of a natural eyebrow flash is pictured below. In real-life situations, it doesn't appear so exaggerated, because it occurs very quickly . . . thus the term "eyebrow *flash*."

"Friendly" eyebrow flashes involve *brief* eye contact with

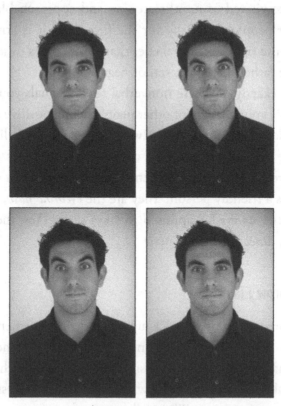

Eyebrow Flash

other persons, particularly if you don't know the person or are a passing acquaintance. Prolonged eye contact between two people indicates intense emotion and is either an act of love or hostility. Prolonged eye contact, or staring, is so disturbing that in normal social encounters we avoid eye contact lasting more than a second or two. Among a crowd of strangers in a public setting, eye contact will generally last only a fraction of a second, and most people will avoid making any eye contact at all.

The Head Tilt

A head tilt to the right or to the left is a nonthreatening gesture. The tilted head exposes one of the carotid arteries, which are positioned on either side of the neck. The carotid arteries are the pathways that supply the brain with oxygenated blood. Severing either carotid artery causes death within minutes. People who feel threatened protect their carotid arteries by tucking their necks into their shoulders. People expose their carotid arteries when they meet people who do not pose a threat.

Head Tilts

A head tilt is a strong friend signal. People who tilt their heads when they interact with others are seen as more trustworthy and attractive. Furthermore, people who tilt their heads toward the person they are talking with are seen as more friendly, kind, and honest as compared with individuals whose heads remain upright when they talk.

It seems that the head tilt has universal "friend" appeal throughout the animal kingdom.

This photo demonstrates the power of the head tilt when seen in dogs. You just assume that the canine in the picture would surely lick your hand if you approached (which, because of the head tilt, the dog is more likely to do).

The Sincere Smile

A smile is a powerful "friend" signal. Smiling faces are judged to be more attractive, more likable, and less dominant. A smile portrays confidence, happiness, even enthusiasm, and, most important, signals acceptance. A smile telegraphs friendliness and increases the attractiveness of the person who is smiling. The mere act of smiling will put people in a better, more receptive mood.

A smile releases endorphins, which give us a sense of well-being. When we smile at other people, it is very difficult for them not to smile back. This return smile causes the target of your smile to feel good about themselves, and if you make people feel good about themselves, they will feel better about you as a person.

The only problem with the smile is what scientists and observant members of the general population have long recognized. There is the "sincere" or "genuine" smile and then there is the "fake" or "forced" smile. The sincere smile is used around people we really want to be more open to elicitation or already know and like. The fake smile, on the other hand, is often used when we are forced by social obligation or the requirements of our job to appear friendly toward another individual or group of individuals.

If you want a person to be more likely to share his or her true thoughts with you, your smiles should be sincere. The telltale signs of a sincere smile are the upturned corners of the mouth and upward movement of the cheeks, accompanied by wrinkling around the edges of the eyes. Unlike sincere smiles, forced

Can you tell which smile is the sincere smile and which one is fake?
If you can't, don't despair. Actually, they're *both* sincere smiles!

smiles tend to be lopsided. For right-handed people, a forced smile tends to be stronger on the right side of the face, and for left-handed people it tends to be stronger on the left. Fake smiles also lack synchrony. They begin later than sincere smiles and taper off in an irregular manner. With a sincere smile the cheeks are raised, bagged skin forms under the eyes, crow's-feet appear around the corners of the eyes, and with some individuals the nose may dip downward. In a fake smile you can see that the corners of the mouth are not upturned and the cheeks are not uplifted to cause wrinkling around the eyes, the telltale sign of a sincere smile. Wrinkling around the eyes is often difficult to see in young people, whose skin is more elastic than older folks. Nonetheless, our brains can spot the difference between a sincere smile and a fake smile.

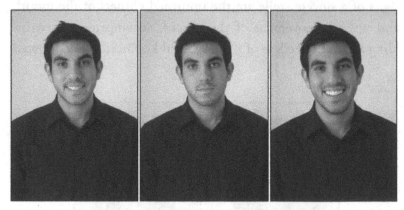

The smile on the left is fake, the smile on the right is sincere,
and the photograph in the middle is neutral.

Remember: the way you smile will influence how effective your elicitation will be. Learning how to produce a "sincere" smile at will, particularly when you don't feel in the mood to do so, takes practice. Study the pictures in the book and think about smiles you have seen in your everyday life. Then stand in front of a mirror and produce fake and sincere smiles. It won't be that difficult. Just think about the times you have genuinely wanted to show appreciation to someone you loved or were forced to smile at some unwanted houseguest at a family dinner or at an obnoxious business associate during a meeting. Practice the sincere smile until it becomes automatic. Then you can choose to use it when you wish.

Will Rogers was once quoted as saying, "You never get a second chance to make a good first impression." When you recall that a person normally notices you before a word is spoken, the importance of these three nonverbal cues becomes obvious. They set the tone for what will lead, hopefully, to a successful elicitation.

APPROACH 2: FOLLOW THE "GOLDEN RULE OF FRIENDSHIP"

Following this rule is the key to all successful relationships, whether they are of short, medium, or long duration. When it is properly employed, it will facilitate the elicitation process by making targeted individuals more prone to providing the information you seek.

The Golden Rule of Friendship

The Golden Rule of Friendship states: *If you want people to like you, make them feel good about themselves.* Do not underestimate the power and importance of this rule in making friends and encouraging people to be truthful during attempted elicitations.

As an FBI special agent, I was required to meet people from every station in life and convince them to provide sensitive information, become spies, or confess to a variety of crimes. The key to the successful completion of these daunting tasks was my ability to get people to like me because I did my best to make them feel good about themselves.

This isn't always easy. One time I was dealing with a suspected pedophile. Having children of my own made it very difficult to act civil toward this suspect, let alone make him feel good about himself. Yet I forced myself to remain nonjudgmental as I questioned him and never threatened him or spoke in anger. When, after several interrogation sessions, he admitted to his crimes, he claimed the only reason he confessed was because I had treated him with respect and not prejudged him concerning the guilt or innocence of his actions.

If every time you meet a person you make them feel good about themselves, they will seek every opportunity to see you again to experience those same good feelings. The stumbling block many of us have in achieving this objective is our own egos. People's egos get in the way of practicing the Golden Rule of Friendship. Most individuals think the world revolves around them and they should be the center of attention. But if you want to appear friendly and attractive to others, you must forgo your ego and pay attention to the other person and his or her needs and circumstances. Other people will like you when you make *them*, not *you*, the focus of attention.

Think about it: it is unfortunate that we seldom use this powerful rule to make ourselves more likable and, at the same time, make other people feel better about themselves. We are too busy focusing on ourselves and not on the people we meet. We put our wants and needs before the wants and needs of others.

The irony of this is that other people will be eager to fulfill *your* wants and needs and, more specifically, be more forthcoming if they like you.

There are several separate rapport-building approaches you can utilize to make people like you. Depending on the circumstances, the person(s) involved, and your comfort level, you may choose to use any or all of these verbal approaches in your pursuit of the truth. With practice, you will become comfortable using one or more of these approaches at a time to establish good rapport while following the Golden Rule of Friendship with your person of interest.

Empathetic Statements

After you establish nonverbal rapport with Approach 1, friend signals, the next step is to use *empathetic statements* to make people feel good about themselves. This is one of the simplest and most powerful elicitation techniques described in this book. These statements keep the focus of the conversation on the person you are talking with rather than on yourself. Empathetic statements such as "You look like you are having a bad day" or "You look happy today" let people know that someone is paying attention to them and cares to some degree about their well-being. This kind of attention makes the recipient feel good about themselves and, more important, predisposes them to like the person who made the remark: the elicitor. As you recall, the foundation of Scharff's interrogation technique was empathy.

Empathetic statements are basically responses to a targeted person's verbal or nonverbal behaviors. Thus the statements encompass several themes. First, you can recognize another person's emotional status ("You look very sad today"). Second is understanding and validating the person's feelings or behavior

("Anger is a natural emotion after what you experienced"). Third is showing the other person respect ("You earned the right to make such a claim"). Fourth is indicating support from the other person's point of view ("Together we can find a solution to the problem").

A common mistake when making empathetic statements is mimicking the language of the person you are speaking with. For example:

> **PERSON OF INTEREST:** My boss is giving me so much work, I can't keep up.
>
> **ELICITOR:** Oh, your boss is giving you so much work you can't keep up.

When using empathetic statements to follow the Golden Rule of Friendship, avoid repeating back word for word what the person said. Since people rarely do this naturally, when it does occur, the repetition is processed by the brain of the listener as abnormal behavior and causes a defensive reaction. This is the exact opposite effect of what you, the elicitor, want to achieve. Parroting another person's statement can also sound patronizing and condescending and even come off as a form of mockery. Don't do it!

In this instance, the communicator is feeling overwhelmed by the amount of work he is required to do. This emotion should be reflected back in *similar* words but not using the *same* words. The following is an example of a good empathetic response to his statement:

> **PERSON OF INTEREST:** My boss is giving me so much work, I can't keep up.

ELICITOR: You feel overwhelmed by the amount of work you are required to do.

Another common mistake that occurs when making empathetic statements is not making the person of interest the focus of the conversation. For example:

PERSON OF INTEREST: My boss is giving me so much work, I can't keep up.

YOU: I know how you feel, because *my* boss gives *me* a lot of work too.

The elicitor did not keep the focus of the conversation on the targeted individual, violating the Golden Rule of Friendship. How can the elicitor know what the person of interest is feeling? The person of interest is the only one who knows that. This could lead to feelings of hostility, expressed in terms like "How do *you* know how I'm feeling? You're not me . . ."

The basic formula for constructing empathetic statements is "So you . . ." There are many ways to form empathetic statements, but this basic formula gets you in the habit of keeping the focus of the conversation on the other person and makes them feel good about themselves. And using empathetic statements is a simple yet effective technique that will have people seeking you out to be their friend, because every time they converse with you, you make them feel better about themselves. And, best of all, they will not know you are using this technique, because people naturally think they deserve the attention and will not see your actions as being out of the ordinary (that is, their brains will not flag such remarks as abnormal or suspicious).

Once you have mastered constructing empathetic statements

using the basic formula, you can make more sophisticated empathetic statements by dropping the "So you . . ." format. That will spark the speaker into commenting further, giving you time to think of something meaningful to say in response. Here are two examples of how you might respond empathetically to a targeted individual's comment, first using the basic "So you . . ." response, then employing a more sophisticated reply:

Example 1

GEORGE: I've been really busy this week.

TOM: So you didn't have much free time in the last few days.

Example 2

GEORGE: I've been really busy this week.

TOM: Free time has been at a premium in the last several days.

A good empathetic statement captures the emotional content of the message. Remember to keep the focus of the conversation on the elicitation target, not yourself, the elicitor.

Empathetic statements also serve as effective conversation fillers, helping to keep conversations going during attempted elicitations. The awkward silence that comes when the other person stops talking and you cannot think of anything to say is devastating. When you are struggling for something to say, fall back on the empathetic statement. Just remember the last thing the person said and construct an empathetic statement based on that information. The speaker will carry the conversation, giving you time to think of something meaningful to say in response.

It is much better to use a series of empathetic statements when you have nothing to say than to say something inappropriate. Remember: the person you are talking to will not realize that you are using empathetic statements because they will be processed as "normal" by the listener's brain and will go unnoticed.

Compliments and Flattery

Another way to apply the Golden Rule of Friendship is to give someone a compliment. The danger is that if the person perceives your compliment as false and/or hiding some ulterior motive, he or she will come away with a negative impression of you. After all, no one likes to feel they are being manipulated or lied to. If you tell someone they are good at something and they know they aren't, they are likely to question your motive, because they recognize the discrepancy between your assessment of them and the way they really are.

However, there is another, vastly superior method of using compliments. This approach avoids the pitfalls inherent in complimenting another person and instead allows targeted individuals to compliment themselves, avoiding the risk of appearing insincere. Sincerity is not an issue when people compliment themselves, and they rarely miss an opportunity to do so. A good elicitor will use that to his or her advantage by providing that opportunity.

The key to allowing people to compliment themselves is to construct a dialogue that predisposes them to recognize their attributes or accomplishments, then give themselves a pat on the back. When people compliment themselves, they feel good about themselves, and according to the Golden Rule of Friendship they will like you because you provided the opportunity to make them feel that way. Here is a typical example of how to get someone to do this:

> **BRAD:** I see you've been really busy at work lately.
>
> **CHRISTINA:** Yeah, I've worked sixty-hour weeks these past three weeks finishing a project.
>
> **BRAD:** It takes a lot of dedication and determination to commit to a project of that magnitude. [Offers Christina the chance to compliment herself.]
>
> **CHRISTINA:** [Thinking.] I sacrificed a lot to get that megaproject done, and I did a very good job if I may say so myself.

Brad allowed Christina to give herself a pat on the back for her hard work, thus making her feel good about herself. And by directing the conversation using a simple empathetic statement, he got Christina to compliment herself without even noticing she had done it.

Compliments come in many shapes and sizes. Almost eighty-five years ago, Dale Carnegie recognized the value of compliments in his book *How to Win Friends and Influence People*. The book is still a bestseller. Why? Because Carnegie was one of the first to recognize and publicize the importance of compliments in accordance with the Golden Rule of Friendship. One of his suggestions was to look at a person and pick out something about that individual that they felt proud of, and then compliment them on it. The reasoning behind this strategy was solid: if they made an effort to "look good" by wearing a specific article of clothing or sporting a well-trimmed mustache, then most likely they would appreciate you noticing this aspect of their physical appearance.

In today's world one must be a bit cautious about complimenting people about their appearance (clothing, hairstyle, body shape, etc.), but when done appropriately and respectfully, it can make individuals feel better about themselves and build rapport, both critical factors in achieving a successful elicitation.

If you don't want to take a chance praising someone on the way they dress or look, there are plenty of other ways you can give out compliments, such as on the occasion of a birthday, an anniversary, the birth of a child, a marriage, a significant civic or social honor, getting a new job, receiving a promotion, joining an organization, achieving success in a vocation or avocation, or buying a new car, house, or other significant product. Even knowing a person's name in cases where it wouldn't be expected can be perceived as a compliment. Mark Twain once said that the sweetest word in the English language was a person's own name. The list goes on and on. Basically, the number of potential compliments you can come up with is pretty much determined by the limits of your own imagination.

Complimenting a person about something works for two reasons: (1) it makes them feel better about themselves and (2) it shows them that you care enough about them to take the time to notice and comment on some aspect of their life. When people think you care about them, they are more inclined to like you. Theodore Roosevelt captured the essence of this perfectly when he stated, "People don't care how much you know until they know how much you care."

When giving compliments, remember to be honest and not to overdo it. Also, compliments need to be believable. As indicated earlier, if you tell a person he or she has done a great job and they know they've been a slacker, your efforts will not end well. In sum, providing a person with the opportunity to like themselves through your compliment will enhance the chances they will like you more as well, creating an environment conducive to the most effective elicitations.

Finding Common Ground

One of the quickest ways to build rapport is to ask someone to discuss something they are interested in. For example, if someone you know is an avid fisherman, you might show an interest in the topic by asking them about it (e.g., "How did you get interested in fishing? What kind of fishing do you like to do? What is the biggest fish you ever caught?"). People *like* to talk about things they care about, and they will *like you* for providing them the opportunity to do so.

When you share "common ground" with another individual, it gives you a natural opening to build rapport. If you see a person wearing a Cubs baseball cap and you're a Cubs fan yourself, it's a natural conversation and friendship starter. Even if you aren't a Cubs fan, you can use the information to see if there is other common ground between you and your person of interest (for example, both of you might like baseball or live in the same city or have opinions about sports betting).

People with similar interests find it much easier to build positive relationships. When you are planning to use elicitation on a specific individual, take a moment to find out if there is anything about that person that would suggest you have common ground for building rapport. Of course, if you meet a person of interest at a social or professional gathering, you may already have common ground to use in building a relationship. If, for example, I'm at an electronics convention or a national meeting of real estate brokers, or attending a rodeo or coin show, and I meet a person of interest at that location . . . well, most likely the "common-ground" approach to building rapport will prove highly successful.

APPROACH 3: BECOME AN ACTIVE LISTENER

Eliciting the truth does no good if you don't hear it. Friendship is a two-way street; don't make it a one-way road! Sadly, for many people, that's what ends up happening. Most of us blithely assume that if someone is within earshot of our voice, they hear what we're saying. Unfortunately, that's not the way it works. Think of how often in your own life you were in a conversation with someone and your mind wandered, and suddenly you realized you have no idea what they just said. Or you meet someone during a social or business event and moments later you can't even remember their name. "In one ear and out the other" is more than a colloquialism; it is a true description of what happens when we hear words but our brain doesn't process them. In other words, we *hear*, but we don't *listen*. This can lead to tragic results. *What good is elicitation if a person reveals the truth but we fail to hear it?* Nothing good—that I can assure you, as we will see in a few moments.

The difficulty in listening, in part, comes from the fact that we can think four times as fast as most people talk, so there is a tendency for us to "tune out" the speaker and tune in to our own thoughts, preventing us from accurately hearing what the other person is saying. Add to that the fact that people engaged in conversation are often so focused on what they want to say that they are oblivious to what the other person is saying. I encounter this problem in my classroom at least once a semester: a student asks a question about the course, I answer the question, and then another student asks the very same question. How can that be? It's because the second student is so concerned with how to phrase his question or simply daydreaming that he doesn't listen to the first student. When a person says something, concentrate on his or her words without thinking about what your question or response will be.

The first step in processing information effectively while practicing elicitation is simply to listen carefully to the person of interest. Failure to listen is probably the most critical weakness in effective communication. If you don't listen attentively, you are liable to miss critical information and be at a loss in framing good follow-up statements to keep the elicitation going.

Good two-way communication takes effort on the parts of both the speaker and the listener; it is not a given. It requires a speaker who knows how to talk and a listener who knows how to pay attention. I will teach you what to say to effectively gain true statements from a person of interest, but, equally important, I want to emphasize your need to *listen* if you want the elicitation process to be most effective.

The good news is that effective listening is a learnable skill—one you'll want to develop, because it is critical not only for effective elicitation but for anyone who wants to engage in successful communication in their everyday lives. Effective listening is referred to as "active" listening, because it is a conscious, committed effort on the listener's part to focus on a speaker while he or she is talking—not daydreaming, not thinking of something to say, or becoming distracted.

It is not easy to actively listen to someone; most of us are not used to doing it. But it will become easier, even second nature, with practice. Here are the components of active listening you will want to master to become an effective communicator and elicitor:

(A) When Someone Is Talking, Concentrate on What They Are Saying

Focus on their words and don't let your mind wander or allow other thoughts to intrude. Failure to listen is the most common and often the most serious communication error. Here's an extreme example of what can happen when a listener's attention lapses.

On June 11, 2007, Larry Craig, a U.S. senator representing the state of Idaho, attracted national attention when he was arrested in a Minneapolis–St. Paul International Airport restroom. It turned out that Senator Craig ended up in the wrong place at the wrong time attempting to do the wrong thing. Specifically, he solicited an undercover police officer for sex. Now, to establish that this illegal behavior had taken place, two "solicitation signals" had to be present: (1) bumping feet with the person in the adjacent stall and (2) sliding a hand along the bottom of the divider separating the stalls. Craig displayed these two solicitation signals to the undercover policeman posing as a willing participant seeking illegal sexual activity, and thus he was arrested.

After Craig was detained, a detective interrogated him about his actions in the restroom. Here is an excerpt from the actual transcript of the conversation.

DETECTIVE: Okay, um, I just wanna start off with ah . . . your side of the story, okay? So, ah . . .

CRAIG: So, I go into the bathroom here as I normally do, I'm a commuter here too.

DETECTIVE: Okay.

CRAIG: I sit down, um, to go to the bathroom and, ah, you said our feet bumped. I believe they did, ah, because I reached down and scooted over and um, the next thing I knew, under the bathroom divider comes a card that says 'Police.' Now, um, (sigh) that's about as far as I can take it, I don't know of anything else. Ah, your foot came toward mine, mine came toward yours, was that natural? I don't know. Did we bump? Yes. I think we did. You said so. I don't disagree with that.

DETECTIVE: Okay. I don't want to get into a pissing match here.

CRAIG: We're not going to.

Do you see the problem here? If you don't, read through the conversation again. You may have missed what the detective missed as well. The detective's problem was he did not actively listen to what Larry Craig said. After the senator described his activities in the bathroom stall, he concluded that he did not disagree with the undercover officer's claim that he had bumped feet with him. The detective's response to this admission clearly shows that he did not listen to what the senator said. The senator reiterated the detective's question—"Did we bump?"—and then answered the question: "Yes, I think we did. You said so. I don't disagree with that." Craig agreed that his feet and the undercover cop's feet bumped; however, the detective did not seem to hear the senator admit to the first action that had to take place for the crime to be committed.

Then things got worse. Later in the interview, the detective attempted to get the senator to admit that his hand came below the divider, the second necessary action that had to take place in order to establish that Craig had committed a crime. The transcript reads:

> DETECTIVE: I will say every person I've had so far has told me the truth. We've been respectful to each other, and then they've gone on their way. And I've never had to bring anybody to jail because everybody's been truthful to me.
>
> CRAIG: I don't want you to take me to jail, and I think . . .
>
> DETECTIVE: I'm not gonna take you to jail as long as you're cooperative, but I'm not gonna lie. We . . .
>
> CRAIG: Did my hand come below the divider? Yes. It did.
>
> DETECTIVE: Okay, sir. We deal with people that lie to us every day.
>
> CRAIG: I'm sure you do.

A cursory glance at the brief conversation between the detective and the senator reveals once again that the law enforcement official was not an active listener! The senator directly admitted that his hand had dipped below the divider, yet the detective was not focusing on what the senator said. Consequently he missed the senator's admission to the second behavior that had to occur for the crime to be committed.

Two months after his bathroom encounter, Craig pleaded guilty to misdemeanor disorderly conduct in the Hennepin County District Court. He was fined $500 and received a ten-day jail sentence, which was suspended. Craig was also given one year of probation. Fortunately, the detective's poor listening skills did not impact the outcome of the case, although one could surmise that Senator Craig might have been left wondering how many times he had to admit to his crime before the detective would hear his admission of guilt.

It never ceases to amaze me how many people, even trained professionals, are not good listeners. Unfortunately, I'm reminded of the problem too many times to ignore it, particularly when the offending parties are my elicitation trainees.

One memorable example comes to mind. I sent several students out to the local shopping mall to see if they could use "bracketing"—an elicitation technique I'll describe later—to get salesclerks to reveal their birth dates. The students worked in pairs so one student could watch and critique the other student as they attempted to complete their assignment. On this day I sent two students into a clothing store to see how they would perform. One of the students was an extrovert (an outgoing, talkative, gregarious type of person), the other an introvert (more introspective and reserved). In general, extroverts talk a lot and listen less, whereas introverts talk less and listen more. At any rate, the extrovert was charged with getting the birth date information, and after chatting with the salesperson for several minutes she finally said, "Thank you" and walked dejectedly out of the store. She turned to her partner, who had listened to the entire exchange, and said, "Wow, I really screwed that up, didn't I? I just couldn't get the information." The introvert shook his head in amazement. "What are you talking about?" he retorted. "You got everything." The extroverted student had been so busy talking to the employee that she never even heard the clerk give up his birth date! Again, the elicitor's inability to listen ended up costing her valuable information.

(B) Once a Person Finishes Speaking, Wait a Second or Two Before Responding

Silence serves several purposes. First, it allows time for the listener to more effectively process what was said before responding. Second, the time lapse allows the speaker to provide additional information that they might not have supplied without the additional break in the conversation. People often feel the need to fill silence gaps, particularly if elicitors nod their heads and use verbal encouragement such as "Uh huh," "Interesting," and "Go on."

Given these extra few seconds of opportunity to speak, people who are predisposed to talk will sometimes volunteer information that one can hardly believe they would willingly provide. Case in point: during one of my shopping center exercises, U.S. Customs and Border Protection officers dressed as civilians were practicing the elicitation skills I had taught them during my four-hour orientation class. One officer was assigned an elicitation target who worked in a novelty shop. The officer was instructed to get the person's date of birth. The officer not only achieved this objective but he was also able to get the salesman's full name as well. After getting the name, the officer paused for a few seconds to see if any other information might be forthcoming. To the officer's amazement, the elicitation target went on to reveal that he had an outstanding arrest warrant for drug possession. He then mentioned that he was in the United States illegally. When the exercise ended, the officer ran the elicitation target's name and date of birth through government databases. Sure enough, there was an active warrant for his arrest for drug use. The officer notified the local police department, whereupon the elicitation target was arrested. When people are predisposed to talk, sometimes they talk too much!

(C) Use Nonverbal Cues to Show the Speaker You Are Interested in What They Are Saying

When speakers notice a person isn't listening, it can stop the flow of information very quickly. The best way to focus on the listener's speech and at the same time convey to the speaker nonverbally that you are paying attention to what they are saying is to maintain eye contact. It is also a friend signal that helps build stronger rapport. You needn't stare at the speaker to accomplish this; however, it's best to maintain eye contact with the speaker about two-thirds to three-fourths of the time they are talking to establish the appropriate degree of connectivity and to indicate you are tuned in. Nodding affirmatively (as opposed to nodding off) and maintaining a posture of interest (you can certainly remember the difference when someone appears interested versus disinterested in what you are saying by observing their body posture) all help transmit an *I'm interested* message to the speaker. This will encourage the speaker to be more willing to talk and provide you with the information you are seeking.

(D) Make a Concentrated Effort *Not* to Interrupt Speakers While They Are Talking

Extroverts must be particularly careful not to do this, as they tend to begin talking before the speaker is finished speaking and, in fact, finish what the person is saying to hurry the conversation along. People like individuals who let them talk, particularly when it is about themselves. Sports announcer Ed Cunningham once observed, "Friends are those rare people who ask how you are and then wait to hear the answer."

(E) Use Empathetic Statements to Demonstrate That You Are Listening to the Speaker

In order to form a good empathetic statement, you must listen to what the person is saying or take note of their emotional or physical state. Paraphrasing what the person has said keeps the focus on that individual.

For example, if you need help in a department store and you observe that the salesperson looks tired, you might not get the service you expect. To increase the chance of getting better service, you could use an empathetic statement such as "You look like you've had a busy day," "It's been a long day," or "Looks like you're ready to go home." Such statements demonstrate to the salesperson that you took the time to notice how they are feeling and, more important, make them feel good about themselves.

Even a dull conversation can be enhanced with empathetic statements. For example, a coworker is talking excitedly about his weekend trip to the lake. Unless you went to the lake with them, the experience might not interest you. An empathetic statement such as "Sounds like you really enjoyed your trip" will let your coworker know that you are listening and taking an interest in what they are saying. Empathetic statements are the spice of conversations. If you make it a habit to use empathetic statements, you will force yourself to listen more carefully to other people. As a result, they will feel good about themselves and like you.

Remember, individuals enjoy talking about themselves and feel good when people listen to them verbalize their thoughts, which brings us back to the Golden Rule of Friendship. When you can make a person feel good about themselves, they are going to be more inclined to like you . . . and tell you the information you are trying to obtain.

A DOCTOR'S ACTIVE LISTENING PRESCRIPTION
FOR BETTER ELICITATIONS

"Building Trust in Less Than 10 Minutes"—that was the title of an article written by an anesthesiologist named Scott Finkelstein published online by the *Huffington Post*. In the article the doctor described what it's like to face life-and-death problems daily and emphasized the importance of doctor-patient communication in dealing with medical crises. "I give each patient my full attention," Dr. Finkelstein explained. "I maintain eye contact. I listen. I validate their feelings . . . The fear melts away. And then they trust me. All in less than ten minutes." Every great elicitor is an active listener who heeds the words of Epictetus, a philosopher who, more than two thousand years ago, provided this insightful wisdom: "We have two ears and one mouth so that we can listen twice as much as we speak."

A FEW THINGS TO REMEMBER

When you enter the "home of elicitation," leave your ego at the door. Most people are egocentric: they think the world revolves around *them*. That self-perception won't fly when it comes to conducting a successful elicitation.

The single most important skill for elicitors to learn is how to suspend their egos during interpersonal interactions, but it is a difficult goal to achieve. Collecting information is not about you, your job title, your professional skills, or your social standing. The focus of any elicitation is all about your targets. The conversation should center on them, their jobs, their professional skills, and their social status. Never forget that to be an active listener, your attention should be focused on hearing and processing what your person of interest is saying . . . not on *you*, *your* opinions, or *your* current emotional state.

If people enjoy your company, they will want to spend more time with you. The more time people spend with you, the more opportunities you will have to steer conversations to the subject matter of your elicitation. That is most likely to happen when the focus of the conversation is on them and not *your ego*.

The tendency for people to be egocentric doesn't just affect their capacity to be effective elicitors; it also spills over into other areas of their lives in a deleterious manner. Consider, for example, this true story from the business world:

Vickie, a recent college graduate, secured a coveted position at a prestigious chemical company. She was a diligent and hard worker who took each task seriously and completed it effectively. She kept up with new developments in her field and always tried to learn the newest and most cost-effective techniques to help strengthen the company's bottom line. One day Vickie discovered an innovative method to reduce the cost of manufacturing a certain chemical. She went to her manager to report her discovery.

"You've been doing this all wrong," she said confidently. "I found a new and cheaper way to manufacture the chemical." Much to her shock and dismay, rather than praise her for her discovery, her manager dismissed Vickie's findings outright and admonished her to concentrate on her assigned work. Crushed, Vickie returned to her cubicle and vowed never to take the initiative again.

It turns out that Vickie's intentions were good, but the way she communicated her idea was not. Her ego set her up for failure. It might have been true that she had found a cheaper way to produce the chemical, but she did not present it in a diplomatic manner that the manager could accept. His reaction to her office visit was predictable: No doubt he thought, *I've been a manager for fifteen years. Who does this inexperienced, snot-nosed college graduate think she is? Get some experience under your belt before you come prancing into my office and tell me I've been doing things wrong for my entire career. Go back to your cubicle and do as you are told.*

In this instance the manager's ego trumped common sense and the all-important bottom-line benefit that would have been realized had he accepted his employee's new manufacturing strategy. Sadly, egos have hurt more people and torpedoed more good ideas than a healthy business environment can really afford.

Instead of saying, "You've been doing this all wrong. I found a new and cheaper way to manufacture the chemical," Vickie should have elevated the status of her manager and elicited his opinion. For example, she could have said: "Sir, I would like your advice on something that might make our company more profitable." The manager's expertise in the subject would then have become a starting point for a constructive discussion of Vickie's recommendation.

It is good for you to develop self-confidence and inner strength, but if a by-product of that development is a big ego, I suggest you leave it at home if you want to be interpersonally effective, particularly when you are dealing with people more powerful than you or during elicitations.

The less a person perceives you as a threat, the more they will like you as an individual and tell you the truth when questioned. You can create such an environment by employing the approaches discussed in this chapter. Not only will they help you become a more effective truth detector, they will also enhance your interpersonal effectiveness with all the people you come into contact with on a daily basis: your family, your work associates, even the multitude of strangers you encounter only once in your life.

CHAPTER 3

Natural Human Behavior: Why Elicitation Is So Effective

Proprietary information can be protected in
locked safes, behind a series of physical and
electronic barriers. The weakest link in any
security chain are humans. Once a lock is
locked, it will not unlock itself . . . but a tied
tongue easily unties itself.

UNKNOWN

In this chapter we'll explore some psychological principles that cause people to reveal information willingly and unknowingly. Elicitation works because it takes advantage of basic human predispositions that, when triggered, kick-start a person's willingness to talk, and talk honestly. Knowing these psychological principles will help you understand why elicitation techniques work so effectively. The basic elicitation techniques we'll be using are based on these reliable, predictable patterns of human behavior. Before we get into these behaviors, let's review one powerful example of elicitation and these principles at work.

THE JEWELRY STORE YOU'LL WANT TO ROB

One thing that never ceases to amaze my students, my FBI trainees, and my corporate clients is how easy it is to acquire sensitive information from targeted individuals using elicitation. Let me give you one example from the thousands I have witnessed.

During one of my elicitation exercises in the shopping mall, I instructed a student to go into a jewelry store, engage the store clerk, and elicit the security measures used in the store. "Imagine you are going to rob the place and want to learn information that will maximize your chances of getting away with the crime," I suggested to my student on our way into the store, where I would pretend to be his friend during the elicitation so I could give him pointers later.

The student went up to one of the display cases to look at some jewelry items. A salesperson came over and greeted him. He responded by saying "Hello" and displaying the "big three" friendship signals—the eyebrow flash, the head tilt, and the sincere smile—to build rapport. He then mentioned that he was looking for a ring to give his girlfriend for her birthday. This led to the following conversation:

STUDENT: Wow, this is nice stuff. I could just put this stuff in my pocket and walk out of the store. ["Presumptive statement," an elicitation technique.]

CLERK: Yeah, I guess you could.

STUDENT: Oh, I see you have cameras. I'd get caught for sure. [Presumptive statement.]

CLERK: Not really. Those are dummy cameras.

STUDENT: *Dummy cameras?* [Feigned or real disbelief, another elicitation technique—in this case real disbelief.]

CLERK: Yeah. They sure look real, don't they?

STUDENT: Well, the mall security officers keep an eagle eye on things. [Presumptive statement.]

CLERK: That's a laugh. I see them about once a day. They just sit in the food court and drink coffee their entire shift.

STUDENT: That leaves you. I don't think you'd chase a shoplifter. [Presumptive statement.]

CLERK: Heck no. My boss told me just to let them go.

STUDENT: Let them go? [Feigned or real disbelief—in this case, real disbelief.]

CLERK: Yeah, the store doesn't even bother reporting shoplifting unless the loss is greater than $1,200.

STUDENT: You mean I could walk out with a thousand-dollar ring in my hand and you wouldn't even report the theft to the police?

CLERK: Yup.

STUDENT: Cash must be a different story, though. [Presumptive statement.]

CLERK: We keep excess cash in the safe. It's mounted in the wall behind the counter over there.

STUDENT: Well, at least the cash is safe. [Presumptive statement.]

CLERK: Not until we fix the safe. It won't close properly.

STUDENT: I can't believe you keep money in a safe that doesn't close properly. [Feigned or real disbelief.]

CLERK: There's $2,200 in the safe now. I put it there a little while ago.

The student switched the conversation to some trivial subjects, told the clerk that he didn't see anything he wanted to buy, and thanked him, and we exited the store.

After the exercise I held a debriefing with the student. He was amazed that the clerk would so readily tell two perfect strangers about the weaknesses in the store's security system. What was equally amazing was that the clerk didn't even realize he had revealed sensitive information. I can assure you that if the student had walked up to the clerk and asked, "How easy would it be to rob your store?" he would not have come away with the information he acquired using elicitation. That's the power of this approach in getting at the truth.

Based on the information the salesperson provided, a shoplifter could walk into the jewelry store, pick out an item or items costing less than $1,200, and leisurely walk out without fear of getting caught *or even reported*—not to mention the possibility of taking $2,200 from the unlocked safe. I seriously considered going back to the store and telling the clerk that he should be more careful when talking to strangers. In the end I decided against it, since we were conducting a covert exercise and I didn't want to compromise our presence or our purpose; also, we intended to use the shopping mall for future exercises.

Like my student, you probably find it hard to believe that an employee of a jewelry store would willingly provide such confidential and critical information. Yet it doesn't surprise me, and the reason is because I have seen it happen so frequently, I've come to view it as expected behavior when elicitation is effectively used.

PEOPLE HAVE A NATURAL TENDENCY TO CORRECT OTHERS

Most people are insecure to one degree or another. Insecurity makes us feel inferior to individuals we think are smarter, richer, or more educated then we are. Insecurity drives us to show others that we are just as smart or smarter than they are. An effective way to prove that we are just as good as or better than others is to correct them when they misspeak or state erroneous information. When we correct others, we elevate ourselves above the person we are speaking with. This makes us feel good about ourselves, serves as a reward for correcting others, and drives us to continue correcting others whenever possible so we can experience that same good feeling again and again.

As we learned in an earlier chapter, just as suppressing your own ego facilitates a successful elicitation, exploiting the ego of the elicitation target plays an important role in obtaining true information.

People typically cannot accept propositions that deflate their egos. This was illustrated in a conversation I had with a colleague from another university. He wanted to find out if a member of his department had received a discretionary increase in her salary and, if so, how much. (These merit increases over base salaries were not publicly announced.) He approached the woman and said, "Hey, rumor has it you didn't receive a discretionary raise . . . That really surprised me." (Presumptive statement.) My colleague expected the woman to either agree with him or—if she *did* get a raise—correct him and satisfy her ego at the same time. In fact she replied, "I did get an increase." At that point my colleague said to her, "I heard they gave out $3,000 to each recipient." (Third-party perspective, an elicitation technique we'll be discussing later.)

"That's not true," she said, shaking her head. "I got twice that." In this way, using elicitation, my friend was able to learn that his colleague had received a bonus and the amount involved. The other professor felt compelled to provide the information without thinking about the consequences of what she was revealing. He ended his elicitation on a good note by allowing his colleague to feel flattered: "I'm not surprised; you really deserved it."

The need to correct is so powerful that even when people are aware of the elicitation technique, they feel an overwhelming need to correct others. I demonstrated the need to correct a student in one of my classes. I asked the student to explain her understanding of the need to correct and its relation to elicitation, and she did. I thanked the student and said, "That was good insight for a sophomore." The student instantly replied, "I'm a sen—" and paused. She gritted her teeth and said, "I can't help myself. I feel an overwhelming need to correct you even though I know what you're up to." Then she blurted out, "I'm a senior!" With great relief she then admitted, "Now I feel better."

Using this technique requires elicitors to suspend their egos. The need to correct others is a double-edged sword. On one edge, people feel a need to correct others. Conversely, people have a hard time saying something they know is obviously wrong. Doing so erodes the ego, which lowers the elicitor's status in relation to the elicitation target. The same psychological principle that compels people to correct others also applies to the elicitor, inhibiting him or her from making intentionally erroneous statements. Remind yourself that it's okay to be wrong. The sun will still rise in the East and set in the West. Your friends and family will still love you. The purpose of elicitation is to obtain information that people would not otherwise reveal—not to boost your ego.

During my lectures, I regularly demonstrate how to make errors in order to be a more effective elicitor. At the beginning of a presentation, I intentionally make several mistakes that do not damage my credibility, such as mispronouncing a word or misspelling one on the whiteboard. The participants immediately correct those small errors. With a show of embarrassment, I graciously accept the corrections and credit the participants for being attentive. This technique accomplishes several objectives. First, the person making the corrections feels good about him- or herself, which builds rapport between the two of us. Second, participants are more likely to spontaneously interact during the lecture without the fear of looking stupid in front of the instructor, the logic being it is okay to make mistakes because the instructor already made several himself. Finally, minor mistakes make me look human. People like lecturers who are experts in the subjects they teach and yet, at the same time, possess human qualities like their own.

PEOPLE HAVE A NATURAL TENDENCY TO TALK ABOUT OTHER PEOPLE

If something does not directly affect us, we tend to talk more freely about it. People like to talk about other people in order to let others know that they are "in the know." In many instances people talk about others because they don't care about the other person and are not worried how the information will be used. In reality, this could be as simple as a company employee overhearing information in the cafeteria about a new product being developed in another division of the company. In order to be competitive, product development is usually kept confidential.

If an employee has no real investment in the new product, they may have little interest in keeping its development a secret, even if they have been told that as much and warned not to share information about it with people outside the company.

PEOPLE HAVE A NEED FOR RECOGNITION

Some people feel a greater need to be recognized than others, but we all welcome recognition for the work we do or the goals we achieve. Receiving a monetary bonus for a job well done or having your name on the company's employee-of-the-month plaque are good ways to be recognized. However, people place more value on the recognition that comes directly from other people, especially close friends, coworkers, and supervisors. A simple compliment on a job well done will often produce a treasure trove of information. Recognition is an indicator that the person being complimented is a cut above the ordinary: they are special. The person being complimented may then provide detailed and often sensitive information to prove themselves worthy of the praise they have received.

People who think they are *not* being given enough recognition for the work they do become prime targets for elicitation and recruitment for espionage. John Charlton was one of these people. Charlton was employed as an engineer at Lockheed Martin's Skunk Works, a classified facility that works on secret government projects. Charlton worked on stealth technology for naval ships. He felt his efforts at work were not appreciated and began surreptitious contacts with several foreign intelligence services to sell classified stealth technology.

The FBI, through sources, found out about Charlton's overtures and set up a sting operation. An FBI undercover agent posing as a transportation expert working for the French government contacted Charlton. During their first meeting, the undercover agent told Charlton his work with stealth technology was innovative and that he was considered an expert in the field. The undercover agent went on to say that Charlton's journal articles were well received worldwide and that he was recognized in France as a genius. Finally, Charlton was getting the recognition that he deserved! In return for this and a cash payoff, Charlton sold the formula for the stealth coating used on the *Sea Shadow*, a secret ship being built for the U.S. Navy. Charlton betrayed his country for financial gain and some well-placed compliments.

Recognition is a powerful motivator. Bartenders, social workers, and empathetic people listen to the real or imagined slights suffered by disgruntled employees, former employees, and unsuccessful job applicants. A sympathetic ear allows people to vent their frustrations, disappointments, and unrequited dreams. During the venting process, people are more vulnerable to being elicited for personal or business secrets.

PEOPLE HAVE A NATURAL TENDENCY TO GOSSIP

People like to gossip. Gossip is information shared about an absent third party. Gossip differs from the human tendency to talk about other people in that gossip tends to focus on negative information to demean people rather than praise them or express envy of them. Gossip typically focuses on negative aspects of a person's appearance, achievements, or behavior. A more benign form of gossip is when people discuss celebrities.

Some people gossip to seek revenge. People who do not like

an individual will typically seek out other people who also dislike that person. Subsequent conversations center on negative evaluations of that person. The enmity for the target of the gossip is validated and justifies hurtful behavior. When people say negative things about others or gloat about their misfortunes, they are secretly relieved that they are not the victims of the same ill will or bad luck.

People also like to gossip because possessing secret information about another person gives them a sense of power. In order to display that power and reinforce their egos, people must share the information. The urge to gossip comes naturally and most of the time gossip is exchanged casually to break up the monotony of routine activities or simply to spice up conversations. Social media is an ideal platform for gossip. Personal attacks on others are posted anonymously. Gossip on social media tends to be more harmful because it has a wide audience and remains visible for a long time. For this reason social media platforms are a good source of passive information about people and activities.

People are predisposed to gossip when they hear the words "Did you hear about [insert target's name] . . . ?" or "I can't believe what [insert target's name] did . . ." In the first case, the lead-in introduces an assertion that, if false, prompts the listener to refute it. In the second case, the lead-in encourages the listener to respond with any information they have to prove that they are "in the know." People want to be seen as being well-informed when it comes to the latest gossip. If knowledge is power, gossip is turbocharged power that energizes elicitation.

PEOPLE ARE NATURALLY CURIOUS

A good elicitor will engage a target's curiosity as a way to get information without having to ask prying questions. When there is an "information gap"—a void between what people know and what they want to know—their curiosity is aroused and they are driven to fill this void. The uncertainty of not knowing something causes anxiety, and people seek to satisfy their curiosity in order to relieve this anxiety, return to a state of equilibrium, and gain closure. Curiosity also has a reward component: satisfying one's curiosity—or filling the information gap—can be a relief. People experience a sense of satisfaction once this objective has been achieved.

When people are curious, they tend to talk more than they listen. This is counterintuitive: one would expect a curious person to listen to other people rather than speak in order to obtain their desired information. But curiosity tends to have the opposite effect: it stimulates people to ask questions and to talk more rather than less. A curious person will often be more open in conversation and exchange information more easily. This has the additional benefit of helping the elicitor build trust with their target, since exchanging information is a common indicator of friendship. People will go to great lengths to satisfy their curiosity, and this desire to satisfy one's curiosity is used by elicitors to extract information. Marketing campaigns are often engineered to boost sales by generating curiosity. For example, one day I walked into a department store, and a person at the door handed me a scratch ticket with three silver circles. I had to scratch one of the silver circles to find out how much I would save on any purchases I made that day. The savings ranged from 5 percent to 50 percent, but the discount would not be honored if more than one circle was scratched off. I recognized the marketing ploy immediately and put the card in my pocket unscratched. Five minutes passed. I could not take the tension. I had to know. I pulled out the scratch card and, using my thumbnail, I scratched one of the circles to reveal a 5 percent discount. I was curious about what lay under the two other circles. I decided to forgo the 5 percent discount to satisfy my curiosity. To my surprise, all three circles read 5 percent. No matter what circle I chose, I would have received a 5 percent discount. This marketing strategy used curiosity to entice shoppers to scratch a discount that was ostensibly up to 50 percent off. Once the customer scratched the silver off the card, they were unlikely to scratch another circle and lose the 5 percent discount they already won. Even a 5 percent discount increased the probability that customers would spend more than they originally intended, because they rationalized they were getting a bargain.

Curiosity is also used to sell clothes. Clothes are folded and stacked in neat rows on tables for two reasons. First, the retailer wants you to touch the garments. If you like the feel of the fabric, then you are more likely to buy it. Second, a folded article of clothing makes a customer wonder what the rest of the garment looks like. In order to find out, the customer must unfold the garment—this time forcing him or her to feel the garment. If the garment feels good to the touch, a sale is more likely. Of course, the opposite is also true: if a garment doesn't feel good to the touch, the customer won't buy it. To increase the chance that customers will touch garments, retailers place small circular cutouts with the words "Touch me," "Feel me," or "Try me."

"Cliff-hangers" in television series are an example of how

curiosity is used to keep viewership high. Curiosity drives television viewers to watch the next episode or the next season to find out how a cliff-hanger is resolved. Once the viewer reengages, he or she is likely to continue watching the series. If not for the cliff-hanger, viewers might fall out of the habit of watching the series. "To be continued" is always a very effective tagline because it arouses curiosity.

PEOPLE HAVE A NATURAL TENDENCY TO RECIPROCATE

Reciprocity is a normal human impulse. When a person receives something—either tangible, like a gift, or intangible, like a favor or advice—from another person, it's natural for him or her to want to respond in kind. Reciprocity is a widely accepted practice that transcends cultural boundaries. In fact, the urge to reciprocate is stronger between strangers than between friends. It is felt most strongly right after the initial gesture of goodwill is made.

People are inclined to reciprocate for a number of reasons. One reason is that they want to convey a positive image. Another reason is that, by reciprocating, they feel that they are inherently good. To reinforce their self-image, people will perform reciprocal acts even if they do not like the person they are interacting with. People also reciprocate because they feel a sense of indebtedness, and they want to do something in return as soon as possible to relieve that sense of indebtedness. Reciprocity is essential to the survival of humanity. People are social beings. They need to help each other in order to perpetuate the species. If I help you survive today, you will help me survive tomorrow. The adage "I'll scratch your back if you scratch mine" has merit.

When I interviewed suspected criminals, I always offered them something to drink. This small gesture is a common tactic used by law enforcement and intelligence personnel to make a suspect want to reciprocate. If I give something to a suspect, he or she will be more disposed to give me something in return. The thing I am hoping for is a confession or privileged information. Similarly, restaurant waitstaff often get higher tips if they include a mint with the food bill. In fact, just signing their name or drawing a happy face on the back of the bill triggers the impulse to reciprocate.

PEOPLE HAVE DIFFICULTY KEEPING SECRETS

Keeping secrets is very hard to do. Ben Franklin observed that three people can keep a secret if two of them are dead. Self-disclosure is another basic human tendency. Information is power. The more information a person knows, the greater the illusion of power becomes. Secrets constitute unique information and therefore equate to even more power. If I know a secret and you do not, then I am more powerful than you are because I possess privileged information you do not. The catch is that the only way people can exert power is to reveal that they have a secret. When practicing elicitation, remember: people usually can't resist sharing secrets if given the chance.

Keeping a secret consists of two parts. First, you must not reveal the fact that you possess secret information, and, second, you must not reveal the secret itself. Telling someone that you have a secret is an ego-rewarding experience. If you do not reveal the fact that you possess secret information, then you cannot exert power over people who do not have that information.

Therefore people may feel the urge to reveal that they are guarding secrets and/or reveal them to prove that they are superior to those who do not guard the same secrets.

Possessing secret information causes anxiety. The secret keeper must maintain a constant vigil to protect the secret. To relieve the anxiety, secret keepers feel compelled to tell someone their secrets. Most people reveal secrets to the people they like and trust. When people reveal secret information, their anxiety over guarding that information is significantly reduced. You can use this to your advantage.

PEOPLE CONSIDER THEMSELVES TO BE EXPERTS IN THEIR FIELDS

Most people take pride in what they do. They like to talk about what they do from one day to the next. They often validate their self-worth by being good employees. If I am good at what I do, then I am a good person. To bolster a good self-image, people talk freely about their professional accomplishments. They may hate their jobs, but rarely do you hear someone say "I really suck at my job" or "I'm really very incompetent at what I do for a living." Because people's identities are strongly linked to their work, they tend to consider themselves experts at what they do. Disparaging a job or employer is one thing, but disparaging their own job performance goes against their instincts, because they are disparaging themselves. In order to demonstrate their expertise, people tend to reveal information that should remain private. Engaging a person about what they do is a powerful elicitation approach, because people have a natural inclination to reveal sensitive information about themselves and their work.

PEOPLE TEND TO UNDERESTIMATE THE VALUE
OF THE INFORMATION THEY POSSESS

The truth doesn't always announce itself in a dramatic reveal like in Jack Nicholson's *A Few Good Men* courtroom speech. Individuals often possess information that they think is of little or no value. What people do not realize is that many pieces of information that seem to have no value individually add up to something of value when taken collectively. (We will see this clearly in an example of corporate espionage presented in Chapter 14.) If a person is not knowledgeable of the larger picture, then they are more apt to reveal the information they do have.

As a counterintelligence officer at the FBI, I made it a point to collect bits and pieces of seemingly insignificant information. In the hands of a skilled analyst, these can reveal a large, detailed picture of what is happening and offer valuable insights. This is particularly true today with the advent of big data-mining efforts on social media. With the personal information gleaned from social media platforms, advertisers can target people who are more likely to use specific products. In one instance, advertisers targeted social media users to identify individuals who fit the profile of a pregnant woman in order to sell them maternity products. Based on social media exchanges and computer searches, the advertisers used a sophisticated algorithm to identify women who are likely to be pregnant. As a result of the advertising campaign, a fourteen-year-old girl's email was deluged by maternity-related products. The girl's father became incensed by the spamming of his daughter's email accounts and made several telephone calls to the company promoting the products to complain about their insensitivity. Several weeks later the girl finally confessed to her father that she was, in fact, pregnant. Bits and pieces of information played a critical role in revealing the truth.

On one occasion, I was called upon to investigate an employee of a defense contractor that worked on classified projects for the government. I interviewed several of the suspect's coworkers. Weaving elicitation techniques into my interviews, I gained bits of information about the suspect's personal habits. The first piece of information I received was that the suspect was a hard worker: he put in long hours during the week and occasionally came in to work on weekends in order to meet tight deadlines. The second bit of information I uncovered was that several times a year the suspect liked to go to Mexico City, where he owned a time-share condominium. The third thing I discovered was that the suspect was eager to learn new skills. In fact, he often talked to people in the company who worked on other classified projects to learn these new skills and offer his advice.

For all practical purposes, the suspect appeared to be a valued employee because of his dedication to work and his collegiality. I provided the fragments of seemingly innocuous information I had gathered to an FBI analyst. When put together, they formed a larger pattern of behavior that suggested espionage. The analyst discovered that a known hostile foreign intelligence officer visited Mexico City at the same time the suspect did. A coincidence? Not in this instance. As it turned out, the suspect stayed late and came in on weekends so that he could copy classified information using the company's copy machine without being observed by other employees. He talked with other employees working on other classified projects not to learn new skills but to gain access to additional classified information he could sell to a foreign government. The seemingly innocuous detail that the suspect visited

Mexico City several times a year was the key to uncovering the suspect's espionage activities.

PEOPLE CAN'T HOLD TWO OPPOSING IDEAS IN THEIR HEADS AT THE SAME TIME

People strive to maintain internal consistency or equilibrium. Cognitive dissonance, or loss of equilibrium, occurs when a person holds two opposing ideas simultaneously. It can also result when people are presented with ideas that are in direct opposition to what they think or believe. Cognitive dissonance causes feelings of discomfort and anxiety. The intensity of cognitive dissonance depends on how highly a person values the opposing perspective; it's greater when the opposing views are personal. The greater the cognitive dissonance, the more pressure a person feels the need to reduce or eliminate it, thereby alleviating his or her anxiety.

This can be accomplished in several ways. First, the person can change his or her beliefs or attitudes. Second, the person can make every attempt to convince other people that their beliefs are not valid. Third, the person can outright dismiss the opposing views as invalid.

Students in my police writing class face cognitive dissonance when they see the grades for their first writing assignments. Often students begin the course thinking they are good report writers. When they see the poor grade on their first assignment, they think, *Maybe I'm not a good writer. My professor sure doesn't think so.* These two opposing perspectives cause cognitive dissonance. At this point, the students have three options to reduce their anxiety: they can spend a lot of time trying to convince me that they are, in fact, good report writers; they can admit they are poor writers and take steps to improve their writing skills; or they can outright dismiss my critique as wrong.

Cognitive dissonance can create strong personal anguish when someone points out they hold two opposing views. Faced with this tension, it is not unusual for someone to reveal important information they would otherwise never admit.

I was teaching a group of undercover agents how to induce cognitive dissonance to elicit information from their targets. One of the female students was skeptical about the technique and requested that I demonstrate it in class. The best way to respond to skepticism is to demonstrate the technique on the skeptical person themselves.

I asked the female student if she was a mom. She proudly told me that she was married with three children. I replied, "That's great. What does it take to be a good mother?" I asked this to establish a baseline of attributes the student believed a good mother should possess. She told me the following: "Be caring, spend time with your children, provide for them, help them with their homework, and listen to them." I then induced cognitive dissonance. I said, "You volunteered for the undercover assignment." She replied, "Yes." I said, "You knew this job required you to be gone from home for long periods of time." Again she replied "Yes." I said, "So you made a conscious choice to be away from your family." Her "Yes" reply trailed off. She paused. "I am a good mom," she said with conviction. She then told me that it's not the quantity of time a parent spends with a child that matters but, rather, the quality of that time. I said with some skepticism, "Really?" She replied, "I like my job. I don't want to be stuck in the house all day. I want to have a life." She stopped abruptly. Tears welled up in her eyes. She came to the realization that she did not fit her own baseline description of a good mom.

In her attempt to rationalize that she was a good mother, this student disclosed personal information that she would not otherwise have revealed in a public forum. Not wanting to further embarrass her, I went back to my lecture and the example I was going to describe before she interrupted me. At the end of my lecture, she came up to me and said, "I really am a good mother." She continued to recite additional reasons why she could be a good mother and follow her dreams at the same time. I reassured her that she was a good mother and thanked her for her service to her country.

SECTION II

YOUR ELICITATION TOOLBOX

CHAPTER 4

How to Perform a Basic Elicitation

I remind myself every morning: Nothing I
say this day will teach me anything.
So if I'm going to learn, I must do it by listening.

LARRY KING

HOW TO CONDUCT AN EFFECTIVE ELICITATION

Hopefully at this point you understand the numerous reasons why people might be willing to tell you the truth during a conversation. The question is: How do you conduct a proper elicitation? There are several steps you can take to become an accomplished elicitor. I am going to list them now. Remember, becoming a proficient elicitor, like any other skill, takes practice and experience. What I do know, from working with individuals from widely different backgrounds, socioeconomic standing, and education, is that anyone with average intelligence can master the skills needed to become an accomplished truth detector.

As you learn and follow my steps below, you may at first feel awkward carrying them out. Don't become discouraged. With practice, the steps will become second nature, automatic; you won't even have to think about them. It's a bit like learning to drive. When you first start out, it's all you can do just to operate the vehicle. As you get more practice under your belt, you begin to broaden your scope beyond the dashboard and get a feeling for dealing with other drivers on the road. Finally, when you've gotten the driving down pat, you can carry on a conversation with a passenger, think about a business or personal problem, and drive on "autopilot," navigating the roads without even thinking about it.

DON'T ASK QUESTIONS

Questions set off a danger signal in the brain and cause people to become defensive. Answering questions consists of two stages: inward mental evaluation of the question and outward response to the inquiry. When a question, especially one seeking sensitive information, is asked, most people think, *Why does the person want to know this?* Or they might wonder, *How can this person use my answer against me?* or *Why is this person being so nosy?* Such inquiries do not portend a successful outcome for an elicitation. If the person being elicited is asked a question and becomes suspicious, he or she will likely produce a lie to satisfy the person asking the question. In addition, questions are one of the parts of a conversation that people tend to remember after the conversation.

To demonstrate this point, I typically select a random person attending one of my training sessions and ask him or her: "How much money do you make?" The response is predictable and universal. The individual hesitates, thinks about how to respond without offending me, and then says, "Not enough."

In American society, asking a person how much money they make is a violation of social etiquette; it is simply not polite. Later in the seminar I "daisy-chained" several elicitation tools to find out how much money the person actually made. This seminar consisted of government employees. I know government employees are hired using the General Schedule (GS) rating. Each job is assigned a GS grade rating from GS-1 to GS-15. Within each GS grade there are ten steps. Government workers receive step increases annually. Using this publicly available information, I was able to elicit the annual salary of the person who failed to answer my direct question, "How much money do you make?" Here is how I did it, using an elicitation technique known as the "presumptive statement." It is one of the elicitation techniques I'll be explaining in later chapters.

ME: I can see we have a lot of experience in the room today. [Looking at my elicitation target.] You must be at least a GS-7. [Presumptive statement.]

STUDENT: What? I'm a GS-11.

ME: Oh, you just got promoted. Congratulations. [Presumptive statement.]

STUDENT: No, I'm a GS-11-5. [The 5 signifies a step that can range from 1 to 10.]

ME: I can tell you have a lot of experience. [Allow the student to feel good about himself.]

During a break in the class I consulted the GS pay scale and determined that the student made $78,861 annually. Where a direct question failed, elicitation succeeded without the student becoming aware that he had readily revealed personal information he would have otherwise kept to himself. The best way to elicit information is to ask nary a question.

Another student learned the lesson of not asking questions during the shopping mall exercise. I instructed him to get the date of birth from a clerk working in a novelty store. The student went into the shop first and I followed a few minutes later to observe his progress and grade his elicitation technique. When I entered the shop, I heard the student peppering the clerk with questions. The clerk became visibly annoyed and said, "Why are you asking me so many questions?" I gave the student a sideways glance and motioned for him to leave the store. The student learned the hard way that questions cause people to become suspicious and go on the defensive.

DETERMINE WHAT YOU WANT TO ACHIEVE WITH THE ELICITATION

In other words, what truth are you seeking? You need to know this so you can keep the conversation on track and know when your objective is met. You will be much more effective if you start off an elicitation knowing what outcome you want and what steps you must take to achieve your objective.

CREATE THE RIGHT ELICITATION ENVIRONMENT

When planting a garden, you must prepare the soil to create the best environment for the seeds to germinate and grow. Rapport prepares the environment for a successful elicitation. Plants need fertilizer to grow, and so it is with elicitation. The elicitation tools serve as fertilizer that favorably predisposes people to tell all they know. Depending on the circumstances, the person involved, and how well you know that individual, you will want to employ one or more of the rapport-building techniques discussed in Chapter 3. As you approach your person of interest, be sure to flash the "big three" friend signals. Remember to employ the "Golden Rule of Friendship" (empathy, compliments) in your conversational exchange when appropriate. Be an active listener and keep the focus of discussion on your target, not yourself (i.e., practice ego suspension).

CREATE AN "ELICITATION SANDWICH"

The "law of primacy and recency" states that a person will most likely remember the first or last part of a conversation rather than what was discussed in the middle. Think about the last time you went on vacation. You can probably recall in detail the beginning of your vacation and the end, while the middle portion tends to become blurred. Thus, by placing your elicitation focus in the middle, between two unrelated topics, it will be least likely to be recalled. This is known as creating the "elicitation sandwich."

Here is an example of how I built an elicitation sandwich while discovering the truth about a major purchase I intended to make.

Several years ago my wife and I were looking to buy a house. We talked to a few people in the area. They told us that the water table was high in some areas and we should make sure the house we purchased was not in an area susceptible to flooding. After looking at several houses, we found one we both liked. We went downstairs to look at the basement. It had been newly remodeled, so we couldn't see any water stains or other telltale signs of flooding. I knew I would have a better chance of getting to the truth using elicitation rather than asking the real estate agent directly if the home had a flooding problem. The conversation went something like this:

ME: My wife and I really like the large kitchen and all-new appliances. [I began the conversation with small talk to avoid alerting the real estate agent to my real conversational purpose. After a few more minutes of small talk, I *pivoted* toward the topic of my elicitation: possible flooding in the basement.]

REAL ESTATE AGENT: It is a beautiful kitchen with lots of room to cook. You guys will really love the basement. It was recently remodeled. [We walked downstairs to the basement and I stepped over to a nearby window.]

ME: I like the way the dirt is built up around the foundation of the house. [With this sentence I pivoted toward the topic of flooding. Dirt built up around the foundation of a house reduces the risk of flooding.]

REAL ESTATE AGENT: As you can see, the basement is well above the water table.

ME: Wow, they sure did a nice job fixing the flood damage. [I inserted an elicitation technique, the presumptive statement, to be discussed later.]

REAL ESTATE AGENT: The owner also installed a new sump pump. [The real estate agent unwittingly revealed the fact that the basement had, in fact, flooded and been remodeled. The word "also" means that in addition to remodeling the basement after a flooding event, the owner installed a sump pump to prevent future flooding. Having obtained the information I wanted, I reverted to more casual conversation about the house.]

ME: The basement would make a great place for a home office. Can we go back upstairs and take another look at the backyard? I'd like to see if there's enough room for a swimming pool or a pass-through grilling station next to the kitchen. [A change in the focus of the conversation, as dictated by the law of primacy and recency.]

Of course, we did not buy the house. Obtaining the sensitive flooding information through elicitation saved my wife and me potentially countless hours of frustration and added expense to repair the basement, which, having flooded at least once, would likely flood again.

THE ELICITATION SANDWICH: A SECOND HELPING

Here's a second example of an elicitation sandwich being effectively employed by one of my students to elicit a bank account PIN number from an unsuspecting salesperson working at a phone kiosk in a shopping mall. Note how she uses the "rapport and pivot" technique to get to her desired topic of conversation . . . and how she uses the elicitation sandwich to help disguise the real purpose of her interaction.

STUDENT: [Walking up to the salesperson, the student displayed an eyebrow flash, head tilt, and a smile to build rapport. The salesperson reciprocated the friend signals.] Looks like a slow day. [The student uses an empathetic statement to reinforce her earlier rapport-building effort.]

SALESPERSON: Yeah, it's kinda slow. I'd rather be super-busy all day. It makes the time go by faster. Are you looking for a new phone?

STUDENT: I'm new to the area and I'm not sure my phone will work here. I'd like your advice on whether or not I should get a new phone. [This allows the salesperson to flatter herself, another elicitation technique to be discussed later.]

SALESPERSON: Let me see your phone. I'll let you know if it will work here or not. [The student hands her phone to the salesperson.]

SALESPERSON: Wow. This is an older phone. Maybe it's time to get a new one.

STUDENT: I'd like to . . . but I have a hard time remembering the PIN numbers for all my devices. [Here the student pivots the conversation toward the elicitation objective of getting the salesperson's bank account PIN number.]

SALESPERSON: Use something that you can easily remember.

STUDENT: Like your birthday. [Makes a presumptive statement, an elicitation tool to be discussed later.]

SALESPERSON: No. I use my wedding anniversary. I use it for everything.

STUDENT: Really! Even for your financial stuff? [Feigned disbelief/presumptive statements.] I was told not to use the same PIN number for everything.

SALESPERSON: No one knows my wedding anniversary except for my husband.

STUDENT: Wow. You look too young to be married. You must have gotten married at nineteen. [Feigned disbelief, allowing salesperson to flatter herself; presumptive statement.]

SALESPERSON: Almost. I got married when I was twenty.

STUDENT: Getting married in the spring is the best time of the year to get married. [Presumptive statement.]

SALESPERSON: Actually, I got married in July.

STUDENT: There must have been real fireworks on your wedding night. [Presumptive statement.]

SALESPERSON: Close. I got married on the fifth.

STUDENT: You must be only married for a couple of years. You look so happy. [Presumptive statement allowing salesperson to flatter herself.]

SALESPERSON: They've been the happiest three years of my life.

STUDENT: I haven't made up my mind about the phone. I think I'll wait and see how this one works out. It's been a pleasure meeting you. I'll keep you in mind when it's time to buy a new phone. [Switches topic back to buying a phone, thus completing the elicitation sandwich: talk about buying a phone, the "top slice of bread" in the sandwich, followed by the elicitation topic, the "meat" of the sandwich, and finishing up with additional talk about the phone purchase, the "bottom slice of bread" in the sandwich.]

Note: Can you figure out the salesperson's PIN number? I'll be revealing it in a few pages.

ONCE YOU HAVE ESTABLISHED RAPPORT WITH YOUR PERSON OF INTEREST, BEGIN YOUR CONVERSATION WITH "SMALL TALK" THAT IS *NOT* RELATED TO THE SUBJECT MATTER YOU WISH TO FOCUS ON

Beginning the conversation with small talk helps to quickly build rapport. Once people like you, they are less likely to go on the defensive when they are asked to provide more sensitive information. Additionally, people tend to remember things they first hear and see. When you begin the conversation with small talk, people tend not to remember what was said during the middle of the conversation. This psychological principle referred to as primacy will be discussed in more detail in a later chapter.

DURING THE CONVERSATION, WHEN THE OPPORTUNITY PRESENTS ITSELF, PIVOT THE FOCUS OF THE CONVERSATION TO THE ELICITATION TOPIC

After rapport has been established, pivot the focus of the conversation to the topic that contains the information you are seeking to learn. One of my students who was having some difficulty obtaining a PIN number from a stranger in the mall exercise asked me to demonstrate how to elicit a PIN number from a target she would select. I agreed. She pointed to a nearby kiosk selling digital movies on CDs, pointed to the attendant, and said, "Get his PIN number." I walked up to the kiosk with the student at my side. I picked up a CD and examined it front and back. Seeing a likely customer, the attendant approached me. The conversation went something like this:

ATTENDANT: See something you like?

ME: I'm looking for a movie.

ATTENDANT: You came to the right place.

ME: You look like you're pretty knowledgeable about movies. [Empathetic statement allowing the attendant to flatter himself.]

ATTENDANT: Yup, top salesperson last year.

ME: This movie doesn't require a password to see it. I have enough trouble remembering all my passwords as it is. I'm an old guy. My memory isn't as good as you young guys. [Pivoting the conversation toward the topic of PIN numbers.]

ATTENDANT: My memory isn't that good, either. I just use one password for all my stuff.

ME: It must be something you'd never forget.

ATTENDANT: I'm a big movie buff. I use the title of my favorite movie.

ME: My favorite movie is *Saving Private Ryan*. [Using the quid pro quo elicitation tool to be discussed later.]

ATTENDANT: Really? My favorite movie is *Moonraker*, the James Bond movie.

ME: I don't really see anything I want to watch. I'll stop back later. [After obtaining the attendant's PIN number, I reverted to small talk.]

ATTENDANT: See ya.

The student was amazed that I was able to elicit the attendant's PIN number in less than three minutes without him realizing that he was revealing very sensitive information. Turning the conversation to the desired topic (pivoting) is the key to a successful elicitation. By the way, the student was able to obtain a PIN number from a stranger later in the exercise.

DEPENDING ON THE CIRCUMSTANCES, USE ONE OR MORE OF THE ELICITATION TECHNIQUES TO GIVE YOU THE BEST CHANCE OF ACQUIRING THE INFORMATION YOU SEEK

As you begin speaking with your person of interest and the conversation unfolds, you will want to use one or more elicitation tactics that are best suited to obtain the desired information. Sometimes the elicitation technique you choose will be dictated by the kind of information you seek, other times by the attitude of your target, and, finally, by your comfort level in using a specific tactic. (Not everyone is equally adept at using all sixteen tactics, nor need they be to accomplish their objective.) No one elicitation tool fits all situations, but for all situations there is an elicitation tool that will work.

There may be times when you will use more than one elicitation tactic in the same conversation to more effectively extract information from your person of interest. You may find yourself switching from one tactic to another because the first one you chose is not working that well. Remember, your person of interest will not be aware of this: properly conducted, elicitations do not arouse suspicions.

Don't be surprised if one or more of the elicitation techniques feels comfortable to you immediately. Others may take more practice getting used to, but I'm confident you'll have no trouble mastering them all. The more techniques in your repertoire, the better you'll be able to pick the one(s) that work the best with the person on the other side of the conversation.

ONCE YOU HAVE OBTAINED THE INFORMATION YOU WANT, FINISH UP YOUR INTERACTION BY MAKING SMALL TALK THAT IS TOTALLY UNRELATED TO THE FOCUS OF THE ELICITATION

By beginning and ending an elicitation on a topic (or topics) un-related to the focus of the conversation, you further disguise your intentions and make it less likely your target will even remember the middle part of the interaction that was so important to you.

SUMMARY

Let's review the interaction between the student and the cell phone salesperson described a few pages back, because I think it will help you see how the elicitation process works and how it is possible that someone can actually give up their bank PIN number and not even realize it.

The student displayed friend signals as she approached the salesperson. The woman reciprocated, letting the student know that she was open to her approach. The student began the conversation with benign small talk. Once rapport was established, the student pivoted toward the elicitation objective by comment-ing on the fact that she had a hard time remembering the PIN numbers for all her devices. The student then introduced a series of elicitation tools to learn that the salesperson used her wedding anniversary as the PIN for all her devices. The student followed through to learn if the salesperson used her wedding anniversary as the PIN for her bank account.

Through casual conversation, the student was able to elicit how old the salesperson was when she got married and the month and date of her wedding. Using a little math, the student could figure out the salesperson's anniversary date. The woman got married when she was twenty. She also revealed that she had been married for three years, which made the salesperson twenty-three years old. The year 2015, the date of the elicitation, minus three years is 2012. The salesperson was married for three years, which means she got married on July 5. The clerk's bank account PIN number is 07052012.

The student ended her conversation with the salesperson by engaging in benign small talk once again and then left. Amazingly, the salesperson revealed her bank account PIN number to a perfect stranger in less than five minutes. If the student had directly asked the woman for her bank account PIN number, do you believe she would have gotten it? Without a doubt the salesperson would have thought she was joking or being incredibly inappropriate. If she thought the student was serious, she would have become very defensive and suspicious. At best, the woman would have lied about her PIN number.

Using elicitation, the student obtained the truth without asking the clerk a single question. The probability that the information the saleswoman provided was the truth was extremely high, because she did not feel threatened and was unaware that she was revealing sensitive, personal information to a perfect stranger.

The examples provided in this chapter show how elicitation works—and that it *does* work. But just how easy is it to become an effective truth detector? As easy as in the previous examples where my students obtained PIN numbers from unsuspecting strangers. The part that intrigued the students most was that they could accomplish this amazing feat after only four hours of classroom instruction.

So does that mean you're ready to go out and hit the elicitation trail? Not quite yet. At this point you're like a novice golfer who knows the basics of the game but has yet to learn how the various clubs and irons in their bag can be used to maximize their performance on the links.

In the chapters that follow, I will be familiarizing you with the various elicitation techniques at your disposal when you are seeking the truth. Each technique will be explained, and examples of actual elicitations using each tool will be presented. Just as a golfer learns how the various irons and clubs affect the flight of the ball in getting to the cup, so, too, will you learn how the various techniques work in getting you to the truth. Once you have this additional information, you will have all the tools you need to draw out honest information—to reach a point where successfully eliciting the truth becomes par for the course.

CHAPTER 5

The Presumptive Statement

A presumption of any fact is, properly, an inferring
of that fact from other facts that are known; it is an
act of reasoning; and much of human knowledge
on all subjects is derived from this source.
REX V. BURDET

The presumptive statement is one of the most crucial, easy-to-use, and effective elicitation techniques at your disposal. It works by taking advantage of the human psychological tendency mentioned in the previous chapter: the need to correct statements a person perceives to be wrong or to affirm statements that are right.

The presumptive statement presents a fact that can be either right or wrong. If the presumptive turns out to be correct, your person of interest will affirm the fact and often provide additional information. If the presumptive statement is incorrect, he or she will typically provide the correct answer, usually accompanied by a detailed explanation. Following are some actual examples of how presumptive statements were used to elicit truthful responses.

DELIVER OR DELAY?

To illustrate how the presumptive statement is used to get accurate information, consider a real business example in which a buyer hears that the company's new supplier has problems with on-time deliveries due to production line failures. The buyer wants to know if the seller can provide a delivery on schedule. The buyer could ask the supplier a direct question: "Can you deliver our order on time?" Because the salesperson doesn't want to lose the sale, he would likely answer, "Sure we can," even if he knows there will be delivery delays.

A better way to obtain the truth is through elicitation using the presumptive statement. The buyer could make a comment such as "I heard your company's solution for the production line delays is reducing your delivery times." The buyer then waits for the salesperson to either confirm the information, deny the information, or discount the information. The advantage of this presumptive statement is that the salesperson might be more willing to respond because he thinks he is only confirming information the buyer already possesses. The salesperson will also be more likely to provide a truthful answer, because, based on the buyer's statement, he can't be sure just how much information the buyer possesses regarding production delays. In the process of confirming, denying, or discounting the presumptive claim, the salesperson is providing the buyer with more information about production delays than he or she would have learned by asking a direct question.

RING OF TRUTH

Recently I wanted to buy my wife a diamond ring, but I did not want to pay retail. In order to negotiate the best price, I had to know the markup on the jewelry in the store where I was going to make the purchase and the salesperson's commission, if any. For obvious reasons this information is closely held. I knew if I asked direct questions, I would not get the answers I needed to negotiate the best price, so I used elicitation.

> **SALESPERSON:** May I help you?
>
> **ME:** Yes. I'm looking for a diamond ring for my wife.
>
> **SALESPERSON:** We have lots of those. Let me show you what we have. [The clerk handed me a ring and I looked it over intently.]
>
> **ME:** How much is this?
>
> **SALESPERSON:** Eight hundred and fifty dollars.
>
> **ME:** Whoooo, the markup must be at least 150 percent. [Presumptive statement.]
>
> **SALESPERSON:** No, it's only 50 percent.
>
> **ME:** And then there's your 15 percent commission. [Presumptive statement.]
>
> **SALESPERSON:** Not that much. I only get 5 percent.
>
> **ME:** I suppose you don't have the authority to give discounts. [Presumptive statement.]
>
> **SALESPERSON:** I am not authorized to give any discounts. Only the manager can approve them.

ME: Ask the manager if he will sell this piece at a 40 percent discount. [I waited patiently as the salesperson went into the back room. She returned a few minutes later.]

SALESPERSON: He said the best he can do is 20 percent if you pay cash.

ME: It's a present for my wife. [Presumptive statement.]

SALESPERSON: No problem. I'll gift wrap it for you. [I not only saved $170 but I got gift wrapping too!]

In this case, using elicitation instead of direct questions yielded valuable information. The markup on the jewelry was 50 percent and the salesperson's commission was 5 percent, which allowed me to negotiate with confidence. Had the salesperson not divulged this information, I would have paid full price. Based on her behavior, she did not realize she had revealed critical and confidential information.

SHOULDERING THE TRUTH

The following excerpt from an interview between an insurance investigator and a claimant demonstrates the effectiveness of presumptive statements once again. The claimant filed a disability claim stemming from an on-the-job slip-and-fall injury that injured his left shoulder and made him unable to work. The insurance investigator discovered that the claimant had previously injured his left shoulder in a snowmobile accident and wanted to know if the earlier injury was a contributing factor to his current injury.

INVESTIGATOR: And what kind of ongoing problems have you had with that left shoulder that are associated with your previous injury?

CLAIMANT: Very few. [The investigator's direct question yielded little relevant information.]

INVESTIGATOR: The recovery process must have been difficult for you. [Presumptive statement.]

CLAIMANT: I reached a point where I overcame the limitations of my previous accident just through hard work and exercise. I continued to heal myself, just continuously working and building up the shoulder again. And I was back to almost 100 percent until this recent job injury, which workmen's comp is not addressing.

INVESTIGATOR: It takes a lot of determination to heal yourself without medical treatment. [Allowing the claimant to flatter himself.] So your previous shoulder injury was almost completely healed. [Presumptive statement.]

CLAIMANT: Yeah.

INVESTIGATOR: You must have been really frustrated to have your shoulder reinjured when it was almost healed. [Presumptive statement.]

CLAIMANT: Yeah. [Becoming angry.] I had a fourth-degree ACL separation and some bone fragments.

INVESTIGATOR: Without medical treatment, that must have really been a struggle for you. [Presumptive statement.]

CLAIMANT: They recommended surgery for the bone fragments and all that, but I wanted to wait and see how it would heal.

INVESTIGATOR: As bad as the injuries were, you decided not to have surgery to correct the problems.

CLAIMANT: Like I said, I healed it by myself.

Through the use of the presumptive statement, the investigator was able to elicit from the claimant the information that he did not receive medical treatment for the injuries he sustained from his snowmobile accident. Furthermore, he learned that the previous ACL injury was not completely healed, as the claimant had stated on his workmen's comp questionnaire.

THE HEARTFELT TRUTH

The following example reminds us once again that people have a natural tendency to correct others. It is rare that an individual will pass up the opportunity to correct a misstatement. The presumptive technique taps into this impulse.

Some doctors are aware that their patients don't always tell the truth, often because they want to downplay various health issues, so the doctors use the presumptive statement to check the veracity of the patient's self-reported health problems. Such is the case in the following exchange between a doctor (whom I trained) and a patient:

DOCTOR: Do you have any history of heart disease in your family?

PATIENT: No, not really. [The doctor senses equivocation.]

DOCTOR: Good, then your parents are both healthy. [Presumptive statement.]

PATIENT: Well, my dad had high cholesterol, but he's taking medicine for it and he feels fine now.

The doctor asked a direct question, and the patient's response was vague, which signaled the need to probe further. The physician used a presumptive statement to coax additional information from the patient. From the patient's perspective, his father did not have heart disease because he took medication and felt healthy. But learning that information helped the doctor better determine his patient's course of treatment (focusing on tests to measure his patient's heart health).

THE SPOTLIGHT EFFECT

One time I used a presumptive statement to trip up a spy. I had originally targeted the young man, who came from a country hostile to America, to "flip" and become a spy for the United States. After building a close relationship with him over several months, he agreed to work with me. He consistently provided valuable information about the hostile country's intelligence service, its agents, and its ongoing intelligence operations. I paid him handsomely for this information. Our relationship flourished over the next year.

Then one day I began to question his loyalty. I recognized that he had used several elicitation techniques on me to obtain information about the FBI's operational methods and techniques to recruit and handle spies, especially from one country in particular. I suspected that he had offered his services to the country, which was the focus of his subtle inquiries. In the espionage business, spies remain loyal to the country that pays the most, and they will often work for several countries at the same time to increase their income. I decided to test his loyalty using a presumptive statement.

I looked up the public telephone number for the embassy of the country that was the focus of his inquiries. I wrote the telephone number on a small piece of paper. One afternoon, while we sat leisurely talking over coffee, I took the piece of paper from my pocket, slowly unfolded it, and slid it across the table. With great confidence I stated, "I see that you've been making some phone calls." [Presumptive statement.] The spy's face blanched. He froze. His shoulders slumped. "So you tapped my phone," he said. I told him that I had suspected for several weeks that he was spying for the country whose embassy's telephone number was on the slip of paper. In truth, I did not know that he had called that country's embassy. However, I did know that he had to contact the other country's intelligence agency to offer them his services. The easiest way to contact the other country's intelligence service was to call the public telephone number of that embassy. The young man was eventually arrested and deported back to his country to face an uncertain fate.

Other psychological factors amplified the power of the presumptive statement I used. One of these factors is known as the spotlight effect. When people lie, they become hypersensitive and believe that the target of their lies knows they are being deceitful when in fact this is often not the case. Another psychological factor working in my favor was the confidence with which I presented the embassy phone number. The spotlight effect enhanced my ability to detect any possibility of deception. I also counted on the fact that he would recognize the embassy's telephone number and that the number would evoke a stress-induced freeze/fight/flight response, thus allowing me to detect nonverbal cues that indicated deception.

I presumed that the young man had thought for some time before deciding to contact the other country's embassy. I assumed that he looked up the number and wrote it down on a piece of paper, looked at it repeatedly, and may have partially dialed the number several times before completing the call. The intensity of the actions surrounding his double cross would have caused him to at least recognize the embassy number if he saw it again and trigger his freeze/fight/flight response.

I combined the presumptive statement technique with an ambush. We were both at ease. We relaxed, drank coffee, and made small talk. Then suddenly, without warning, I became very serious. If the young man had denied calling the number, I would have merely shrugged my shoulders and said, "Just curious." He might have protested, but I would have sent the message that I was watching him closely, which might have preempted him from entertaining thoughts of being disloyal in the future.

THE PRESUMPTIVE QUESTION

Elicitation is typically done without asking any questions. Yet some people feel the need to ask them. In most cases, asking questions is not recommended in eliciting information, as it tends to put people on guard. However, carefully constructed questions, depending on the situation, should still allow you to obtain useful information. If you must ask questions, ask ones that are more likely to elicit truthful answers.

Presumptive questions increase the probability of obtaining honest answers. They present facts that are either true or false. The presumptive question is an option to use when you assume the person you are talking to knows the answer to the inquiry.

When presented with a presumptive question, your person of interest will either confirm the presumption or make corrections if the presumption is wrong. The presumptive question places the person in a position where a nonresponse affirms the presumption or forces the person to provide additional information to correct the presumption. The spotlight effect is at work here as well: the presumptive question gives the illusion that you, the interviewer, possess more knowledge than you actually do.

When presented with two options, liars feel obligated to pick one of the two options. People who tell the truth have a universe of answers to choose from and do not feel obligated to select one of the two possible answers implied by your question.

I routinely used presumptive questions when I interviewed suspects. Instead of asking the general question "Do you know Levi?" I asked the presumptive question "When was the last time you met with Levi?" Asking the general question "Do you know Levi?" gives the suspect an opportunity to lie by simply responding, "I don't know Levi." Asking the presumptive question "When was the last time you met with Levi?" assumes that I know for a fact that the suspect knows Levi. The suspect is less likely to lie when asked a presumptive question.

Presumptive questions can be used in business environments to increase the probability of honest answers. For example, a supervisor wants to know how often an employee uses his office computer for personal business while on the job. The supervisor could ask the question "Do you use your computer for personal business while on the job?" This general question allows the employee to lie or obfuscate the truth by simply responding, "No, I don't use my computer for personal business." The presumptive question "How many times a week do you use your office computer for personal business?" is a more difficult question for the employee to answer because the presumptive question pre-supposes that the supervisor knows for a fact that the employee uses his office computer for personal business. The employee is less likely to lie when confronted with a presumptive question.

In another example, a negotiator suspects the company he is dealing with has legal problems and wants to know if those prob-lems will affect the company's ability to fill an order. Asking the general question "Does your company have any legal problems?" leaves wiggle room for deception. The presumptive question "Are the legal issues your company is facing going to affect your ability to fill our order?" reduces the probability of deception because the respondent assumes the person asking the question possesses information about the legal issues facing the company when in fact the person may not. You can construct presumptive ques-tions to encompass any topic that you want in order to increase the probability of getting closer to the truth.

THE ESCAPE CLAUSE

The following example demonstrates how parents can use elici-tation to obtain sensitive information about their kids' behavior. When using the presumptive approach with your children, you should always have an escape clause. This escape clause allows you to retreat without losing parental authority and/or being left with an angry child who thinks you don't believe him or her. In this case we're going to use a modification of the presumptive statement and replace it with the presumptive question.

Instead of asking your son "Do you use drugs?" ask him, "When was the last time you used drugs?" The presumptive question places your son in a dilemma. It gives the illusion that you know more about your son's drug use than he might have suspected. Your son's reaction to this presumptive question may shed light on his drug use. If he does not use drugs, he will likely proclaim his innocence and express anger that you would think he did. In this event you reply, "Of course you don't use drugs. You are much wiser than your age." This response is an escape clause; it allows the parent to retreat from the initial supposition and allows the child to flatter themselves without feeling any affront from the exchange. If, on the other hand, your son does use drugs, then he will likely hesitate when he answers the question because he must decide if you really possess knowledge about his drug use. If he does hesitate, follow up with a second presumptive question: "Did you really think I wouldn't find out?" This second presumptive question places your son in an even more difficult dilemma. If he answers "Yes," then he admits to drug use. If he answers "No," then he admits to drug use. The only acceptable answer is "Find out about what?"

TAG QUESTIONS

Tag questions turn a statement into a question by adding interrogative tags, such as "isn't it?" or "aren't you?" or "didn't you?" Tag questions are used to confirm known information or to reveal hidden information. I learned the power of tag questions when I bought used cars at the beginning of my career.

The buyer is often at the mercy of the seller, since the seller knows everything about the product being sold, and the buyer often knows nothing about it. The first few times I bought used cars, I later discovered some major problems the sellers had failed to disclose. After these experiences, I learned to ask presumptive questions to get to the truth. For example, I lifted the hood on one car to inspect the engine. The first thing I noticed was that the engine was spotless. Not a drop of oil or a speck of dirt clung to the engine or the other components. I immediately became suspicious. Either the car owner was very meticulous about cleaning the car, or the engine leaked oil and the owner cleaned it to hide the oil leaks. When I looked under the car, I noticed the garage floor had also been scrubbed clean—another clue to the condition of the engine. To get to the truth, I asked the owner a presumptive tag question: "You are going to fix the oil leaks in the engine before you sell me the car, aren't you?" In a low voice the owner said, "It only leaks a little bit of oil." Armed with this information, I was in a strong negotiating position. I could ask the owner for a steep discount on the price of the car, since the engine leaked oil, or I could simply walk away and look for a car with an engine that didn't leak any oil.

NEGATIVE PRESUMPTIVE QUESTIONS

There is one other time when you can use questions to elicit the truth, and that involves asking *negative* presumptive questions. Asking negative presumptive questions elicits the truth more than asking positive presumptive questions or general questions because negative presumptive questions assume a problem exists. A positive presumptive question presupposes that a problem does not exist, allowing the person to provide a vague answer to the question or ignore the question altogether. A neutral presumptive question makes no assumption one way or the other. So how does a negative assumption question work?

Consider what happened with my wife and me when we were

on another house-hunting excursion. We have lived in several different houses during our marriage, and in this case we found one we really liked. But there was a problem, and it wasn't the house. It turned out that the home was located two lots down from a popular fast-food restaurant. Having been a teenager myself, I remembered how my friends and I hung out in the parking lot of a similar fast-food restaurant every weekend. The result: on any given weekend, about fifty rowdy teenagers loitered in the parking lot. And if that wasn't enough to disturb the peace, car tires were constantly squealing as teens drove in and out of the parking lot in a display of raging teenage testosterone. The din continued until 1:00 a.m., when the restaurant closed.

My wife and I wanted to know if there were similar problems with the fast-food restaurant near the home we wanted to purchase. To find out, we could ask the real estate agent a direct, neutral presumptive question: "Is the neighborhood quiet on the weekends?" The real estate agent would simply answer, "This is a quiet neighborhood." This answer does not provide any clues to the truthfulness of the real estate agent, because the question can be answered in a variety of ways to avoid the truth without lying. We could also ask the real estate agent a positive presumptive tag question: "I trust there are no problems with teenagers hanging out at the fast-food restaurant on the weekends, right?" This question presumes that a problem does not exist. The real estate agent could simply answer, "No problems that I know of." This question assumes that we do not know anything about whether a problem does indeed exist. The solution is to ask the real estate agent a negative presumptive question: "Do you think the noise from the teens hanging out at the fast-food restaurant on the weekends will be a nuisance?" People have a difficult time lying when they are asked negative presumptive questions. In this instance, the real estate agent did not know if we were aware of the problems at the fast-food restaurant or not. The negative presumptive question gave the illusion that we possessed specific knowledge about noise pollution coming from the fast-food restaurant when, in fact, we had no definite knowledge of it.

The real estate agent proved to be very honest. Her answer was "I'm not sure. I suggest you come back on the weekend, park in front of the house, and monitor the noise coming from the fast-food restaurant. If it's too noisy, we can always find you another home more suitable for your needs." We took the real estate agent's advice. After one weekend night parked in front of the house, we decided to look for another house in a quieter neighborhood.

The negative presumptive question can be used in a variety of business and social settings. It is equally effective in both oral and electronic communication. For example, if you are buying used items off Craigslist or eBay, asking a negative presumptive question will predispose the seller to reveal any defects in the product. The negative presumptive question is also effective during negotiations. To illustrate, if you are bargaining for a critical part and require on-time delivery but do not know how reliable the manufacturer is, you could ask the negative presumptive question "Have your assembly line problems been solved yet?" The sales representative will likely tell the truth because he or she is not sure how much information you possess and will not likely take a chance getting caught in a lie.

CHAPTER 6

The Third-Party Perspective

A smart person knows how to talk. A wise
person knows when to be silent.
ROY T. BENNETT, INSPIRATIONAL WRITER

The *third-party perspective* is an elicitation tool used to discover what people really think about sensitive topics—thoughts they normally wouldn't reveal or would lie about if asked in a more direct manner. It is the technique of framing information and facts in the third person. For example, if a husband wants to purchase a new fishing boat, he could frame the contemplated purchase from a third-party perspective, "A friend of mine just bought a new fishing boat," to see how his wife might feel about his own purchase of a new fishing boat. This technique exploits people's natural tendency to talk about other people. People tend to believe information they hear from a third-party perspective, especially when they are being complimented. Hearing things from a third-party perspective gives the illusion that the information must be true because it is coming from a disinterested person.

When you ask people direct questions about sensitive topics such as "Would you cheat on your spouse?" they usually defer to social norms to frame their answer. Social norms are the standards of society that define acceptable and unacceptable beliefs and behaviors. People are expected to adhere to these standards or risk being seen as deviant. Thus, if you directly ask your loved one what they think about cheating, they will turn to social norms for their answer even if it's not what they really think (unless their behavior and social norms are in synchrony).

IS YOUR LOVED ONE PREDISPOSED TO CHEAT?

Everyone wants to know if their loved one is likely to cheat on them. If you ask your significant other if they would do such a thing, rarely will you hear, "Yeah, I don't have any problem with cheating on you." They may *think* that, but they would surely not say it out loud. When you ask people direct questions, they tend to become defensive and ask themselves, *Why do you want to know?* or *How are you going to use this information?* or *Why are you prying into my private life?*

To find out what your loved one *really* thinks about sensitive topics like cheating, do so from a third-person perspective. Instead of asking directly "What do you think about cheating?" make a third-party inquiry: "My friend Sophia caught her husband cheating. What do you think about that?"

When a person is confronted with a third-party observation, they tend to look inside themselves to find the answer and tell you what they really think. The answer you want to hear is "Cheating is wrong. I would never do that to you." However, be prepared for answers such as "Everybody cheats nowadays" or "If a wife can't take care of her husband's needs, what is he supposed to do?" or "If my wife treated me the same way she treated him,

I'd cheat on her too" or "It's no wonder. They haven't been getting along for a long time." These answers tend to reflect what a person really thinks about cheating. In this case the person thinks cheating is acceptable under certain conditions and is therefore open to being unfaithful when certain conditions are met. These responses are not conclusive proof of cheating, but they do provide an indication of the person's propensity for adultery.

WEIGHING THE EVIDENCE

A student told me of an eye-opening incident. She was in a serious relationship with a young man and contemplating marriage. She struggled with a weight problem and exercised regularly to keep in shape. However, she knew that she would eventually put on pounds as she aged or if she were to become pregnant. She wanted to know how her boyfriend would feel if she did gain weight.

One evening they were watching the TV show *The Biggest Loser*, which focuses on obese people and how much weight they can lose in a fixed amount of time. Halfway through the show, her boyfriend blurted out, "If my wife ever got like that, I'd kick her to the curb."

The woman was taken aback. Her boyfriend was revealing his true feelings about overweight women based on a third party's obesity. She decided to test him by asking a direct question: "Honey, if I became overweight, would you kick me to the curb?" Predictably he replied, "No, way. I'd love you no matter how much you weighed." By taking advantage of the third-party-perspective technique—my student hadn't planned it out but was smart enough to learn from it when it occurred—she found out how her boyfriend would really feel if she were to gain weight. She eventually broke up with him and found a more compatible mate.

WHERE THERE'S SMOKE, THERE'S (SOMETIMES) A LIAR

The third-party perspective can be used very effectively when determining if your child is telling the truth. One problem with this approach—or any other one, for that matter—is a parent's inclination to firmly believe their child would never lie to them. Several years ago I wrote a short book on how parents can elicit the truth from their kids (Schafer, 2010*). One of the biggest pushbacks I received for my efforts was a group of angry parents who repeated the same mantra: "My children don't lie. We're such good friends with our kids, they wouldn't lie to us."

Sadly, my informal research indicates otherwise. When I ask my college-age students, "Do you have a close relationship with your parents?" almost all of them answer in the affirmative. When I follow up with "Do you ever lie to your parents?" there's a lot of giggling, and almost every student raises their hand. When I then ask, "Why do you lie to your parents even though you have such a good relationship with them?" they invariably answer, "Because we don't want them to know what we're doing; they wouldn't approve of it."

Given that information, let's say you wanted to know if your son or daughter uses marijuana. If you ask your child a direct question such as "Do you smoke weed?" the child will refer to

---

* J. Schafer, *Fibs to Facts: A Guide to Effective Communication* (Alexandria, VA: Spiradula Press, 2010).

social norms to form his or her answer, which will probably be something like "Marijuana use is very bad. I wouldn't smoke it."

To test your child on what they really think about marijuana use, utilizing the third-party approach, you should say something to the effect of "A colleague at work told me that his son was caught smoking marijuana at school. What's your take on that?" The answers you don't want to hear are: "He shouldn't have brought marijuana to school," "It's only marijuana," and "It's no big deal, marijuana is legal in a lot of states." The answer you *do* want to hear is "It's not right to smoke marijuana at school or, for that matter, anywhere else." When the child is asked about an external event—what some third party has said—he or she is more likely to express his or her real thoughts, opinions, or feelings, because they are talking about another person and not themselves.

I SPY WITH MY THIRD-PERSON EYE

Spies are prone to sell their services to the highest bidder. I always wondered if the people I recruited to commit espionage on behalf of the United States remained loyal to America or to their home country. If I asked them directly if they would change their loyalty if they were offered more money from another foreign country, the answer would be a resounding "No!" This answer may or may not be the truth. I chose elicitation to get to the truth before the recruited spy had a chance to get to the lie. I used the third-party approach. Our conversation went like this:

> ME: One of my colleagues has a friend who is helping us
> like you are. He decided he no longer wanted to work

with us because we were not paying him enough
money. He offered his services to the highest bidder.
What do you think about that?

SPY: If he wasn't getting the money he thought he should be
getting, then I don't see a problem.

This answer troubled me. Since the situation I presented to
the spy was a third-party scenario, he looked inside himself for
the answer. Without realizing what he said, he revealed that if
I didn't give him the money he thought he deserved, he would
sell his services to anyone who would pay more for his services. I
would have preferred it if the spy said something to the effect of
"I am loyal to you, and no amount of money would cause me to
betray you." But he didn't. From that day forward I monitored
the spy's activities very closely, knowing that his loyalty was for
sale.

A STAPLE RESPONSE FROM THE BUSINESS WORLD

The third-person-perspective tactic can be used in a business
situation as well. As an example, let's assume a manager suspects
one of her employees is taking office supplies home or wants
to know if an employee is predisposed to do so. Elicitation can
provide an answer. If the manager chooses to directly ask the
employee if they are pilfering office supplies, they will undoubt-
edly answer, "Of course not." However, if the employee is asked
to comment on a third-person scenario involving a worker from
another company who took office supplies home, he or she is
more likely to tell the truth. The exchange would go something
like this:

MANAGER: A friend of mine who works at another
company is having a problem with employees taking
office supplies home. What do you think of that?

EMPLOYEE: I think that anyone who takes what doesn't
belong to them is wrong and should be disciplined.

The employee's answer came from her heart, since she was commenting on a third-party behavior. This means her answer was highly likely to be truthful.

USING THE STORYTELLING APPROACH TO GET TO THE TRUTH

Storytelling is a more advanced elicitation technique using the third-party perspective. When people hear stories, they often subconsciously insert themselves into the story. To be effective, the story should be relevant to your targeted individual's current situation, have a moral, and suggest a course of action that would encourage the person to tell the truth.

As an FBI special agent, I used storytelling, when appropriate, while interviewing persons suspected of committing crimes. In one investigation a bank teller's cash drawer came up short. She was missing several thousand dollars. Since the bank was federally insured, the bank examiner reported the theft to the FBI. The teller had been previously interviewed by her immediate supervisor and the bank examiner. The teller stuck to her story that she didn't know how the money had gone missing.

Since the teller had already been interviewed twice without success, I chose to use a less threatening, more relaxed interview approach. I started off our interaction by telling her a story about my sister, who, coincidentally, had been a bank teller at one time.

I began: "Let me tell you a story before we get started on the interview. My sister was a teller. She got into a money crunch. She fell behind in her rent payment and several other utility bills. This was on a Friday. To avoid having her electricity and phone service turned off, she needed to pay her bills in full by close of business on Friday. She was expecting her paycheck to arrive in the mail on Saturday, the following day. She decided to take the money out of her bank drawer to pay her bills. My sister figured that she could easily replace the money when she went to work on Monday, and no one would be the wiser. It was a good plan except she did not receive the expected check on Saturday. On Monday, her immediate supervisor asked her why her drawer did not balance. My sister denied taking the money. Her immediate supervisor called the bank examiner. The bank examiner interviewed my sister, and she again denied taking the money. The bank examiner referred the case to the FBI. Before the FBI interview, my sister called me, knowing I was an FBI special agent. She wanted me to help her get out of the jam she was in. Sadly, I had to tell her she was in too deep and there was nothing I could do. I told her that if she would have told the truth to her immediate supervisor or the bank examiner, she would have certainly lost her job, but she would not be facing time in prison. At this point I looked directly into the teller's eyes and paused for a few moments. Then I concluded by saying, "Don't make the same mistake my sister did."

After a minute or so of hand-wringing, tears spilled from the bank employee's eyes. She admitted taking the money and went to great lengths to explain that she was not a thief but, out of desperation, took the money to pay her overdue bills.

The story I told the teller had a moral and suggested course of action that encouraged a truthful response. The moral was to always tell the truth. And the course of action was: If you do lie at first, tell the truth as soon as possible thereafter to avoid getting into deeper trouble.

Here's another example of the storytelling approach used by a doctor to help two of his patients avoid potentially life-threatening problems. In the case of the first patient, the doctor suspected the man might have heart issues, based on family history and blood work, and used a story to get the reluctant patient started on the right course of treatment.

DOCTOR: Do you have any health issues I should know about?

PATIENT: No, nothing I can think of.

DOCTOR: Good. I'm glad nothing is bothering you. I wish that was the case with all my patients. I don't know why, but some of them are reluctant to provide me with complete medical histories or symptoms they are experiencing. Let me tell you a story about a sad case. I had a patient once who was very private and decided, for whatever reasons, to withhold information about a medical condition she had. I ended up treating the symptoms of the medical condition and not the condition itself. She suffered for several years before I could properly diagnose and treat her medical condition.

The doctor paused and then said directly to the patient:

DOCTOR: Mr. Smith [not his real name], if you can think of anything else I should know about your medical history or any unusual symptoms or other medical problems, let me know. I don't want you to end up suffering needlessly.

The story had a moral: full medical disclosure could prevent a potential long-term physical problem and, given appropriate information, could be more successfully dealt with and possibly even prevented. The doctor gave the patient the option to provide additional information during a future visit. This option gave the patient a way to reveal his symptoms later to avoid possible embarrassment from withholding information during the present visit.

In the second case, an empathetic story was told to a patient with a family history of cancer to encourage the patient to undergo an uncomfortable diagnostic test that could detect the disease in its early, most curable stage.

> DOCTOR: You just turned fifty. Isn't it about time for a colonoscopy screening?
>
> PATIENT: I'll take a pass on that, Doc. I feel fine.
>
> DOCTOR: I'm glad that you feel healthy, but let me tell you a story. I had a patient not too long ago who opted not to get a colonoscopy screening because he felt well. Three years later I had to tell him the sad news that he had colon cancer. The cancer was aggressive and spread rapidly. There wasn't much I could do for him. He died six months later. If we had caught the cancer sooner, I could have saved his life.

The doctor paused and looked at his patient.

> DOCTOR: Mr. Smith, I don't want that same thing to happen to you. If you change your mind, let me know.

Again the doctor told a story that had a moral: early detection saves lives and provided a course of action—getting a colonoscopy—to increase the odds of detecting and surviving colon cancer. After hearing the doctor's story, the patient decided to get colonoscopy screening on a regular basis.

Storytelling makes a person of interest more receptive and enhances the chances that they will admit to the truth and will take the actions you recommend. Since storytelling comes from a third-party perspective, people are more apt to disclose the truth.

A storytelling approach to veracity is most effective when the person of interest can see from the content of the story how it would benefit him or her to do what you suggest. In the case of the patient and the doctor, the story pointed out how postponing a diagnostic procedure had led to a person's death and was sufficiently persuasive to get the patient to consent to a colonoscopy. In my case, the story I told revealed the increasingly severe consequences for continuing to lie about stealing money from a bank. It, too, was convincing enough to get the guilty party to realize that continued dishonesty would only worsen the situation and led to her truthful admission of guilt.

The use of storytelling to get people to admit the truth—sometimes to themselves about themselves—is frequently used in dealing with addicts, such as when AA members tell their stories to encourage other alcoholics to admit they have a problem and commit to sobriety. Storytelling is also used by parents who, when they suspect their children are lying about doing dangerous things (smoking, careless or drunk driving, unsafe sex), describe the tragic outcomes they themselves experienced through such behaviors in the hope it might get more honesty from and a cessation of those behaviors in their sons and daughters.

CHAPTER 7

Bracketing: I've Got Your Number

Be interested and interesting. People will be more
interested in you when you are interested in them. If
you want to impress, talk to them about . . . them.
SUSAN C. YOUNG, MOTIVATIONAL SPEAKER

Bracketing is a specialized type of elicitation tool used to discover the truth about something that involves numbers or dates. It is based on the human need to correct others. It is often employed in business in determining deals and the truth about deadlines. We first ran across a bracketing example when I attempted to get the best possible price for a diamond ring. (See page 94.)

The goal of bracketing is to get the elicitation target to provide you with a specific number or date within the bracketing range you present. To do so, your upper and lower brackets must be realistic. If the width of the bracket is too small, then the specific number is close enough that the elicitation target does not feel the need to make a correction. A bracket width that is too wide renders the proposition nonsensical and could cause an adverse reaction. For example, during an elicitation exercise, a student was instructed to elicit a store clerk's date of birth. The student asked me to demonstrate the bracketing technique. I approached the clerk. I engaged in some small talk and pivoted toward age. I casually mentioned that I was too old to wear the clothes for sale in the shop. I said, "You know what I mean. You are closer to my age . . . fifty-five to sixty years old." The clerk's eyes widened. She blurted out, "I'm only forty years old! Do you think I look that old?" Predictably, the conversation deteriorated from there. I had made the mistake of making the bracket too high. Knowing that some people are age-sensitive, I would have been better served making the bracket too low than too high. A low bracket will appear as a compliment. A high bracket comes off as an insult. This experience served as a good object lesson for the student and a reminder to me as well.

Bracketing can also be used to encourage a person of interest to speak with you about a topic you want to discuss. For example, at the appropriate moment during my elicitation classes, I introduce the topic of my favorite actresses. I casually mention that my favorite actress is Sandra Bullock. A few minutes later I reveal that my third favorite actress is Rachel McAdams. After setting my bracket, I move on to the next topic.

Sometimes it takes minutes and sometimes it takes hours, but it *will* happen. A student will ask me who my second favorite actress is. When asked, I tell the students that my goal was to get someone to ask me who my second favorite actress was by using elicitation. I explain that I set up a bracket that induced curiosity. As I discussed in Chapter 3, when people are curious, they typically take actions to satisfy their curiosity. I then resume my lecture. The students interrupt me and ask, "Well, who *is* your second favorite actress?" I smile and remind them that curiosity compels them to find out the answer, even after being told that they were set up. That's the power of elicitation. (By the way, my second favorite actress is Reese Witherspoon.)

AN APPLE A DAY KEEPS THE DISCOUNTS IN PLAY

Bracketing is often used by savvy consumers to get the best possible bargain on items they purchase. One of the best examples was also one of the most surprising: a discount on a new Apple laptop. As one of my assignments at the shopping mall, I instructed my students to choose a store and determine if they gave discounts, how much, and who needed to authorize them. I expected that some stores would give a price break but that others would have a fixed price with no room for negotiation. The Apple computer store was one establishment that I believed would not budge on their list prices. I was wrong, as the following conversation between one of my students and an Apple salesperson demonstrates:

STUDENT: [Walking up to a salesperson, giving the friend signals, and looking at the computers displayed on the shelf.] These laptop computers are nice.

SALESPERSON: What were you thinking of getting?

STUDENT: One of these. [Points to a specific laptop.] You must be able to give a 15 percent discount if I buy it.

SALESPERSON: No, only 10 percent. Only supervisors can give more.

STUDENT: Like 25 to 30 percent?

SALESPERSON: I don't think they can go higher than 15 to 20 percent.

Had the student not found out about the discount through bracketing, it is doubtful the salesperson would have offered her any reduction and instead would have charged the full amount on the price tag.

Now, Apple might have changed their sales practices, or maybe this one store had a special discount policy, but if not, each of you readers who are considering the purchase of an Apple computer can now go into the store and save 10 percent—well over ten times the cost of this book!

HOW LOW CAN YOU GO?

What's remarkable about elicitation techniques is that they work cross-culturally—they are not limited to the United States—because people share the same core set of human behaviors. During an elicitation training class I taught overseas, the students wanted to have an end-of-term party. However, their budget was restricted. Restaurant owners typically give discounts for large groups. So we turned this end-of-year party into an exercise; the challenge was to get the biggest discount a restaurant would offer.

Directly asking restaurant owners what their group discount was did not ensure the students would be quoted the best possible price. In many foreign countries, prices are open to negotiation, and restaurant owners may give a higher "lowest price" than the actual lowest price they would accept. Elicitation, rather than direct inquiries, would provide a more favorable lowest price.

The students were instructed to select five restaurants where they were willing to have the party. With ten students in the class, they paired up and chose a restaurant to visit and solicit prices from the owner. Using bracketing techniques (e.g., "I heard you give large groups a 30 to 40 percent deduction off the meal price"), each pair of students tried to get the best deal they could.

The class discovered that the highest discount for group functions was 30 percent. The restaurant they most wanted to dine at offered a maximum discount of 25 percent, but the fact that a competitor offered a 30 percent discount made them confident they could get the same discount at their preferred restaurant as well.

Armed with their discount information from the five restaurants, two different students approached the restaurant the class preferred and began negotiating a group price with the owner. He readily offered a 10 percent discount. The student negotiators hemmed and hawed. The owner countered with 20 percent. The students pressed for the 30 percent discount, mentioning that other restaurants gave such a discount. The owner hesitated for a moment and then agreed to the 30 percent discount. The cost of the party was now within the students' budget. Had they not taken the time to use bracketing to discover the various restaurant discounts, the party would have cost substantially more.

I BID YOU NOT

Bracketing is especially useful in a business setting because business involves numbers, estimates, and projections. Bracketing is a less invasive means to get to the real number you want to know. In the following example, Bill and George are attending a trade show. They work in the same industry but for different companies, which are bidding on the same lucrative government contract. Bill wants to glean some information from George about the bid his company plans to submit.

> **BILL:** I heard that your company is bidding on the government contract. I don't think your company is big enough to handle the contract. [Presumptive statement.]

> **GEORGE:** We may not be as big as your company, but we recently purchased new equipment and introduced some substantial cost-cutting measures.

> **BILL:** Even so, you can't cut costs by more than 5 to 10 percent. [Bracketing.]

> **GEORGE:** Would you believe 20 percent? We are cutting our margins thin to make sure we win the contract.

Unknowingly, George just provided Bill with valuable information about the rival company's bid. Based on what George said, Bill's company will have to provide a leaner-than-usual bid to secure the contract.

As mentioned earlier, bracketing is best used when trying to find out numbers and dates and can be used to discover personal and/or financial information, such as birth dates, PIN numbers, or various other numbers relating to sale prices or operating costs. Unfortunately, it has become a favorite elicitation tool among knowledgeable scammers who use it to subtly extract information like a person's Social Security number, phone number, bank PIN number, address, and credit score. This information can then be used for identity theft and/or other forms of nefarious behavior designed to take advantage of the unsuspecting victim who gave up the critical information.

CHAPTER 8

Curiosity: The Truth Lure

Curiosity is only vanity. We usually only want to
know something so we can talk about it.
BLAISE PASCAL

I have already discussed curiosity (in Chapter 3) as a basic motivator that drives human behavior. Specifically, curiosity drives people to fill the information gap between what they know and what they want to know. When people are curious, they are also more likely to reveal information that could be useful to know. Thus, elicitors use curiosity to attract, build rapport with, and get information or compliance from persons of interest.

I already mentioned how marketing and advertising professionals use curiosity to encourage consumers to spend more money or buy a specific product. Hollywood has mastered the curiosity hook to catch people's interest and, through "cliffhangers," keep their viewership coming back for more. Perhaps the best example of targeting curiosity to maintain viewer loyalty and generate "buzz" around a television series dates to 1980. That's when J. R. Ewing was shot in the final episode of *Dallas*, a popular adult soap opera in its third season, creating months of curiosity buildup as viewers tried to guess the identity of the assailant. You can use curiosity to "connect" with persons of interest and also as a way to get information from them. Let me give you a few examples in which I used curiosity to catch a spy and gain valuable information on how to fix the telephone system in my office.

THE CASE OF THE CURIOUS SPY

One day at the office, I got a call from FBI headquarters notifying me that Mr. Kim (not his real name), a suspected North Korean intelligence officer, was operating a small business in my area of operation. My objective was to recruit Mr. Kim to become a double agent. A double agent is a person who works for country A's intelligence by spying on country B. At some point country B's intelligence service identifies and recruits country A's intelligence officer to work for country B's intelligence service and spy on country A without their knowledge. Good double agents can provide invaluable information because they have easy access to the intelligence operations of the service they ostensibly work for. Double agents must be monitored very closely because their loyalty is for sale.

The problem was: How could I meet Mr. Kim and get him interested enough to hear my proposal before he got scared and dropped off the grid or denied any kind of espionage work for *any* country? I decided that the use of the curiosity tactic was my best way to gain Mr. Kim's attention, personal interaction, and hopefully cooperation.

I put my strategy into motion by first going to Mr. Kim's shop when I knew he was not there and left a note that read, "Sorry

I missed you. Jack." I did this to pique Mr. Kim's curiosity. Several weeks later I returned to Mr. Kim's place of business when I knew he was gone and left a second message that read, "Sorry I missed you again. Jack Schafer." The second note was designed to further heighten Mr. Kim's curiosity while making me look nonthreatening.

Two weeks passed. I returned to Mr. Kim's shop a third time, again with the knowledge that he wasn't there. This time I left him a note that read "Sorry I missed you. Jack Schafer. XXX-XXXX [my phone number]." Within minutes of leaving the shop, Mr. Kim called me. This was critical, because I wanted him to initiate the first contact.

I returned to Mr. Kim's shop and surveilled the building from the parking lot. I waited until things got busy before walking in. I introduced myself to Mr. Kim and presented my FBI credentials. I looked around the store and commented, "I see you're busy. I'll come back when things aren't so hectic." I turned and left the store. I did this because I knew Mr. Kim's freeze/fight/flight response would engage and he would not be able to logically process information.

An hour later I returned to Mr. Kim's shop and invited him to join me for coffee at a nearby fast-food restaurant. I did this for several reasons. First, I wanted to force him off his personal turf and into a more neutral environment. Additionally, a fast-food restaurant offered the safety of a public place. I suggested that we walk to the restaurant, because when people walk or stroll together, they are predisposed to talk. During the short walk, I began the rapport-building process.

When we arrived at the restaurant, I offered to buy Mr. Kim a cup of coffee. I did this to invoke the human need to reciprocate. (See Chapter 3.) I also chose to interview Mr. Kim over a cup of coffee because, like strolling, people are predisposed to talk over food or drink. In fact, 70 percent of all information is exchanged over a drink or a meal.

After I developed rapport with Mr. Kim, he asked what I wanted from him. I replied, "Mr. Kim, *you* are the one who called *me*. You must have something you want to talk to me about. Why don't we talk about what *you* wanted to talk to *me* about?" Mr. Kim did not realize that he was motivated by curiosity, which was the elicitation tool I used to induce him to call me. I designed my interview with Mr. Kim very carefully using a series of elicitation techniques to motivate him to do what I wanted him to do without him knowing that he was being manipulated.

USING CURIOSITY TO GAIN INFORMATION

One morning a telephone repairman came to the FBI office to install a new telephone system. Since the office was a secured facility, I was assigned to stay with the man until he completed his work. When the repairman opened the telephone control box, I was amazed at the complexity of the crisscrossing wires and cables. I wanted to know how the telephone system worked. Rather than asking the repairman direct questions, I decided to use the curiosity elicitation tool to engage his cooperation in explaining to me exactly what he was doing. The conversation went something like this.

> ME: I'm glad to see you're here on time. I've got a lot of things to do today and need to get back to my work when you're done.

REPAIRMAN: I know the rules. I've worked in several FBI offices. This won't take long. [The repairman walked to the central telephone box located in the storeroom of the FBI office and opened the box. I peered inside and saw a jumble of wires and cables.]

ME: It must take a lot of training and expertise to figure out that tangle of wires. [Giving him a chance to flatter himself.]

REPAIRMAN: No, not really. A telephone is nothing more than a switch. You lift the receiver and you make the connection.

ME: Really? Well, it doesn't look that simple. I'm curious about how it works. Would it distract you if I watched what you did?

REPAIRMAN: No. [The repairman pointed to one side of the connecting bar.] These are the wires coming in from the main hub. [The wires were inserted into separate slots on the connecting bar.] Each wire represents an available telephone line. Directly opposite each incoming line on the connecting bar is a specific extension. [The repairman snapped the wire from one of our five extensions into the first set of slots on the connector bar. I noticed he used a special tool to accomplish it.]

ME: I notice you just used a tool to snap the wires in place. That tool must be specially made to do the job. [Presumptive statement.]

REPAIRMAN: You can use a flat screwdriver to snap in the wires. This tool just makes it easier.

ME: Oh, I see. [The repairman snapped in the last set of wires, printed the last four numbers of the extension

next to the paired connections, and closed the
telephone box.]

REPAIRMAN: All set. I'll let you get back to work. I have to
be at another job in less than half an hour.

ME: Thanks for letting me watch and explaining what you
were doing. [Allowing him to flatter himself again.]

About a year later the information I elicited from the telephone repairman proved invaluable. We decided to rearrange the office. Each of the five agents wanted to sit at different desks. After settling into our new desks, I began getting phone calls for one of the other agents and other agents began receiving phone calls for me. We quickly realized that we had changed desks but not our phone extensions to our new locations. I submitted a work order to have a telephone repairman come out and change the extensions. My supervisor denied the request and told us to notify people that our telephone numbers had changed.

Well, this was unacceptable. We thought about several options. During this brainstorming session, I remembered the time when the telephone repairman came to the office to set up the extensions. I went into the storeroom and opened the telephone box. I no longer saw a tangled jumble of cables and wires. I observed a well-organized set of switches, each labeled with the last four numbers of a telephone extension.

I didn't have a flat screwdriver, so I used the swinging metal file attached to my fingernail clippers. One at a time, using the end of the file, I disconnected the wires leading to each telephone extension and reconnected them to their appropriate new extensions. It worked like a charm. My office mates were astounded at my extensive knowledge of the telephone system. I nodded and told them it was all in a day's work. I never did reveal how I had obtained my "extensive" knowledge of the telephone system, nor did I tell them how easy the procedure was.

I have saved thousands of dollars over the years learning how to fix washing machines, dryers, dishwashers, coffeemakers, and other household machinery. The first time something broke, I would have to call a repairman to have the broken item fixed. Each time one showed up, I made it a point to be present. Using various elicitation techniques, often the curiosity tactic used at the FBI office, I learned how to repair a wide range of household appliances. In fact, I was able to fix almost anything that broke down around the house. I even offered to help some of my friends fix their broken items, saving them hundreds of dollars in repair bills.

CLOSING THE INFORMATION GAP

As we saw earlier, people's curiosity drives them to close the information gap between what they know and what they don't. A curiosity trap can be set by saying or doing something that triggers curiosity. Clothing can serve this purpose. A T-shirt that bears a sports logo or an unusual saying can create sufficient curiosity to motivate a person to approach you. If you know your elicitation target, you can intentionally say something or wear a piece of clothing that will pique the elicitation target's interest. The elicitation target is likely to initiate a conversation based on the common ground you share. This creates instant rapport. The only decision you have to make now is what elicitation tool you are going to use to obtain the information you desire.

I often used curiosity as a tool when I interviewed suspects who were reluctant to speak with me. On one occasion a suspect who was not under arrest at the time of the interview threatened to stop the interview and go home. As he began to get up, I casually said, "Do you want to know what's going to happen next?" He looked at me and tilted his head. He thought for a few seconds and sat down. "Yes," he said, "I would like to know what's going to happen next." I continued the interview. Eventually, using additional elicitation tools, the suspect confessed. I had effectively used curiosity to get the suspect back into the conversation. If I hadn't tapped into the power of curiosity, I would not have gotten a confession.

Employing curiosity to elicit information does take some planning. With a little practice, you will be able to set curiosity traps on the fly.

CHAPTER 9

Status Manipulation

Just because you shot Jesse James
don't make you Jesse James.
MIKE EHRMANTRAUT IN *BREAKING BAD*

Status manipulation is done by ascribing either a higher or a lower status to an elicitation target. In the case of status elevation, the target knows that they do not have the talent to live up to the elicitor's expectations or wants to make a convincing argument that they are worthy of a higher status. This disparity induces cognitive dissonance.

As I pointed out in Chapter 3, the need for recognition is a basic aspect of human nature, and the skillful elicitor can use it to gain truthful information from people who would otherwise remain silent or deceptive. Every individual has their own perception of what their status level is at work and in other areas of daily life. When you, as an elicitor, give a person recognition or a compliment, it triggers the Golden Rule of Friendship, builds rapport, and makes the person more likely to provide you with truthful information. When you elevate a person's status to a level they are not sure they deserve, it can create a need to "prove" to you your assessment is correct, leading targeted individuals to be even more forthcoming with information you seek. The same is true when you deflate a person's status to a level below their perceived level. To show you they are better than your evaluation of them, they will often give up valuable information in the process.

Status deflation works well when dealing with narcissists or people who have a high opinion of themselves. Any deflation of their status will cause them to provide additional information to prove the elicitor wrong. Status elevation works well with people who are insecure or don't like to talk about themselves or their accomplishments. Status elevation is especially effective on low-level government workers or low-level private sector employees. Any status elevation of these people will induce the elicitation targets to either provide reasons why the elicitor's evaluation is not merited or try to justify their elevated status.

I want to provide you with some examples of how status manipulation has been used in the past to facilitate truth detection. Once you study these real-life events, you will be in a better position to employ the technique in your elicitation endeavors.

Imagine that you are a scientist with a top secret clearance who is working as a contractor for the Department of Defense. One day you receive a telephone call from a government official from the Chinese embassy. He invites you to China to give a lecture on some of your unclassified research. All your expenses will be paid by the Chinese government. You report this invitation to your security officer, who tells you that you can give a lecture in China if you don't discuss classified information. You call to confirm your attendance and the Chinese official invites you to come a week earlier so you can do some sightseeing. You agree. You are very excited because this is a once-in-a-lifetime opportunity.

When you land in China, you are met at the airport by a representative from the Chinese government who informs you that he will be your guide and translator for your entire trip. Each morning the guide meets you at your hotel and has breakfast with you. You spend all day sightseeing. The guide buys all your meals and arranges some evening social activities. He is friendly and shares information about his family and social activities. You reciprocate by sharing information about your own family— nothing important, just the names of your wife and children, their birthdays, your wedding anniversary, and the holidays you and your family celebrate. As the days go by, you are amazed that you and your guide have so much in common despite stark cultural differences.

The day of the lecture arrives. The lecture hall is filled to capacity. Your lecture is well received. At the end of the lecture, one of the participants approaches you and says he is very interested in your research. He tells you that your work is fascinating and innovative. He poses a question about the work he has been doing that relates to your research. The answer requires you to reveal sensitive but not classified information. You gladly provide the information along with a lengthy explanation even though it borders on classified.

While you are waiting to board your plane back to the United States, your guide informs you that your lecture was a tremendous success and that the Chinese government would like to invite you back next year to present another lecture. Since the small lecture hall was filled, the guide informs you you'll be speaking in the Grand Ballroom next year. Oh, and by the way, your wife is invited to accompany you, all expenses paid.

As an FBI counterintelligence officer, I was required to debrief scientists who went overseas to determine if they were approached by foreign intelligence officers seeking classified information. I interviewed many scientists who described stories similar to the one above. They all reported that the Chinese were impeccable hosts and never asked about any classified information. No foul play. Case closed.

But was it?

It turns out that the Chinese intelligence officers are excellent elicitors. They skillfully used status elevation, flattery, recognition, and compliments to get information they wanted. Each scientist who was invited to China was treated like a VIP and received copious praise for their work. ("This year the lecture hall; next year the Grand Ballroom!") Their lecture was applauded. Their research was called significant and innovative.

What interested me the most was that, after interviewing several scientists, I noticed a pattern. During the conference a Chinese scientist would approach his American counterpart, cultivate rapport, and then ask for advice on a project they were working on. After reviewing the document, the American scientist would naturally expound on the topic in the form of a lecture. Additionally, the American scientist wanted to demonstrate their expertise on the topic. Unwittingly the American scientist provided information previously unknown to the Chinese scientist. And as the Chinese scientist continued to praise the American's work and probe further, even more information was received in return.

The information provided by the scientist in and of itself was not critical. However, Chinese intelligence officers elicited information from *hundreds* of American scientists through status elevation. The myriad bits and pieces of information formed a larger blueprint of critical technology. As though they were putting a jigsaw puzzle together, the Chinese elicitors were gathering intelligence one piece at a time and then fitting the pieces together to form a coherent picture of technological advancements they did not possess. In the end I made sure to brief scientists before they went to China to be aware of the subtle techniques the Chinese use to steal our country's secrets.

When individuals receive praise for their work, they are more susceptible to liking the person offering the compliments and more willing to share information with them, often unaware of what they are saying as they bask in the glow of recognition. As an elicitor, you can enhance your elicitation effectiveness by taking a page from the Chinese information-gathering playbook.

STATUS ELEVATION = BETTER INFORMATION

I discovered this status elevation technique one day when my son, Bryan, and I went to a bookstore. An author was signing books at a booth in the front of the store. There were no people at the booth, so Bryan and I went over to talk with her. While Bryan engaged in small talk with the author, I looked through her book. I made an offhand remark that her writing style reminded me of Jane Austen's.

The author's eyes lit up and her cheeks took on a pinkish hue. She replied, "Really? I don't have much time to write. I have three kids. My husband is in the military and is gone a lot of the time. I want to go back to college to finish my degree. I left school to get married. That was a mistake I'll always regret." With eager nods and several empathetic statements from me to encourage her to keep speaking, she told me her life's story, including some sensitive information she wouldn't have offered in response to a direct question.

USING YOUR STATUS TO ELEVATE SOMEONE ELSE'S

In 1996, I was assigned to investigate federal civil rights violations in the Antelope Valley. Antelope Valley is located sixty-five miles north of downtown Los Angeles. The two major cities in the Valley are Lancaster and Palmdale. Between 1995 and 1997 a white supremacist gang calling themselves the Nazi Low Riders (NLR) committed a series of high-profile hate crimes. NLR membership numbered about fifty individuals who referred to themselves as "skinheads" and "peckerwoods." They boasted a deep-seated hatred for Jews, African Americans, and Asians.

The incident that triggered my involvement took place in early 1996. Three gang members stabbed an African American student in the back with a screwdriver on the Antelope Valley High School campus. The stabbing was motivated by hate. Shortly after that, an African American teenager was slashed with a machete by several skinheads. The teenager and his female cousin were walking to her home in Lancaster when three men driving by yelled "White power!" and gave a Nazi-style salute. The cousins tried to flee, but they were chased down and attacked.

I wasn't certain how to proceed. My expertise was in counter-espionage operations. I caught spies. I knew nothing about investigating civil rights violations. I consulted a few of my colleagues on how to investigate skinhead gangs. They advised me to conduct extensive surveillance, recruit sources within the gang, or infiltrate the gang using an undercover agent. After considering the usual investigative techniques, I decided to take a more direct approach: I would find out where the gang hung out, go there, and personally gain information about the skinheads using elicitation techniques.

The Nazi Low Riders hung out in a dilapidated house close to downtown Lancaster. Dressed in my best suit, sunglasses, and wing-tip shoes, I loudly knocked on the front door of the clubhouse. A young man about nineteen years old with a shaved head answered the door.

"What do you want?" the skinhead asked in a menacing tone.

I replied with all the authority I could muster that my name was Jack Schafer and I was a special agent with the FBI. The skinhead softened his tone.

"Are you here to arrest me?" he asked.

"No," I said, "I just want to talk to you. Are you a skinhead?" The skinhead nodded tentatively.

I asked, "Are there any more skinheads in the house?" The young man nodded again. I firmly ordered the skinhead to tell the other gang members in the house to come out onto the porch. About six skinheads came out and joined us. I told them who I was and that I wanted to let them know that the FBI was investigating civil rights crimes in Antelope Valley. I also told them that I knew that their gang was responsible for most of the racial violence in the area. I looked each skinhead in the eyes and told them that my job was to put them in jail. I asked them if they understood that my goal was to incarcerate them. They all nodded in the affirmative.

After my stern warning, I softened the tone of the conversation and began to elicit information. I told the skinheads that I was a counterespionage agent and knew nothing about the skinhead ideology. I added that I was interested in learning more about the white supremacist movement. Several of the skinheads took turns informing me that they believed in the supremacy of the white race over "inferior" races. They further informed me that they believed in the separation of the races and that minorities were not welcome in Antelope Valley. This was important information, because one of the elements needed to prosecute federal hate crimes is intent to deprive minorities of their civil rights. Without realizing what they had said, the gang members had helped me establish intent.

From that point on, I made it a priority to talk with as many skinheads as possible to glean additional evidence to prosecute them for their crimes. I talked to four or five of them each day. I asked them few if any questions about their skinhead activities. Instead, I focused on their personal lives. I wanted to know what motivated them to hate so intensely. I spent about an hour a day talking one-on-one to as many gang members as possible. I dubbed these interviews "health and welfare checks."

After about six health and welfare checks, I went to the house of a skinhead whom I had not talked to previously. When he answered the door, I identified myself. The skinhead told me that he did not want to talk to me. I told him that he didn't have to talk to me unless he wanted to. I followed this up with "Do you know the names of any *real* skinheads?" I explained that I only wanted to talk to real skinheads who were proud of their white race and weren't afraid to say so.

The skinhead paused and said, "Well, *I'm* a real skinhead."

I said, "Good, then come out onto the porch and tell me about what you think." He agreed and provided me with more than enough information to prove the intent necessary to establish civil rights violations. I thanked him and told him I would visit him from time to time to see how he was getting along.

After interviewing additional gang members on separate occasions, I went to the home of one I had not yet visited. I rang the doorbell. The skinhead answered. I began to identify myself. The skinhead interrupted me and said, "I know who you are and I'm glad you came."

I was taken aback.

"You see," the skinhead continued, "there is a group of skinheads within the gang who consider themselves real skinheads because they were interviewed by the FBI, and now I can join that group."

My "health and welfare checks" had unintentionally increased the status of certain members of the gang! Without much prompting, the skinhead happily shared his white supremacist ideology and told me about his participation in several crimes, even identifying the people who had committed the crimes with him! Such is the power of status elevation as an information-gathering elicitation tool.

ELEVATING A CUSTOMER'S STATUS TO MAKE A SALE

I was confronted with an issue of status elevation in my own office. As a professor at Western Illinois University, I am approached by sales representatives from major publishing houses who want me to adopt their "latest, greatest" textbook for my students. On one occasion a sales rep showed up at my office unannounced. She wanted me to review a new textbook. She proudly proclaimed the textbook her publisher offered was far superior to the one I was currently using in my class.

I thought to myself, *This woman just told me that the textbook I chose for my students is inferior*. In truth, the book she was touting might have been better, but I was focused on defending my textbook selection instead of looking at the one she was selling. I politely told her that I was satisfied with the textbook I was using and was not interested in her product.

After she left, I paused for a moment to examine why I had bristled at the opening line of her sales pitch. The sales representative's unstated assumption was that I had made a bad decision when I selected the textbook I currently used. Once I began reacting to that, I had no interest in reviewing her textbook, much less adopting it. I thought for a while and came up with a simple opening line that would persuade professors to at least look at a new textbook. Then, if the new textbook was better than the one in use, the odds of a sale would go up dramatically.

Status elevation was the answer to the sales rep's pitch. The opening line needed to go like this, "Hi, Professor [insert last name], I'd like your advice about a new textbook we've just put out if you have the time." Now, instead of selling the textbook to the professor, the sales representative is eliciting the professor's opinion about the product. The salutation "Hi, Professor——" is respectful and recognizes the status of the person she wants as a client. The words "I'd like your advice" elevates the professor's status. The professor will think, *Of course the sales representative would ask me for my advice: I'm a learned professor.* The tagline "if you have time" reinforces the professor's status because time for people with high status is valuable.

This opening line increases the odds that the professor will at least look at the textbook. Looking at the book gives the professor the opportunity to discover for himself whether the book is better than the one he is currently using. If the new textbook is in fact superior, the professor will say so. The professor's opinion serves as a starting point to begin the sales pitch. By elevating the professor's status, the sales rep significantly increases the probability that he will adopt her textbook.

The next time the sales rep came to my office, I asked for her advice on the opening line of a sales pitch I was working on. She readily agreed to listen to my pitch. After hearing it, she thought for a minute and told me my opening line was excellent. In fact, she asked me if she could use it. I agreed instantly.

Several months later the sales representative made a return visit to my office. She happily informed me that the new sales pitch opening line increased the number of professors who reviewed the textbook, and consequently her sales increased as well.

This sales pitch opening line can be adapted to a wide variety of products. Eliciting the client's opinion of a product will yield a more truthful and willing evaluation without putting pressure on him or her to make a purchase. The client's opinion then serves as a starting point for the sales pitch. It turns out that using status elevation has many benefits: it can be a useful tool in the elicitation process, and it can also be used as a business tool to increase sales.

STATUS DEMOTION: IT GAINS INFORMATION BUT CAN DISTRESS THE PERSON OF INTEREST

Once I discovered the power of status elevation after my encounter with the author in the bookstore, I tried the opposite approach with a friend who was a die-hard Democrat. After making some political statements, I told my friend that some of the things he said sounded a lot like what Ronald Reagan stood for. My friend fired back vehemently, "I'm no Republican." He then went on to spend the next ten minutes trying to convince me that he was not a Republican, which he thought was beneath his status. In doing so, my friend revealed a lot about his financial situation that he normally would not have shared if he wasn't so busy trying to convince me he wasn't a "rich Republican."

ADVERSARY OR ADVISER

Two other examples mentioned earlier in the book are relevant to status demotion and what happens when it occurs. Remember Vickie in the previously mentioned chemical case? She approached her boss with her idea to improve production, boldly claiming she had it right and he didn't. Result? Vickie was sent back to her office with a stern warning to get back to her job and let the manager do his. In the case of John Charlton, his perceived lack of status in his job at Lockheed Martin's Skunk Works made him willing to sell top secret stealth technology to foreign intelligence services.

There is no question that the use of status demotion, intended or otherwise, can create an environment where one can successfully elicit critical information, but, in the process, the use of the technique can negatively impact the self-esteem of the intended person of interest. This collateral damage should always be considered before undertaking status demotion as an elicitation technique.

WHY DOES STATUS ELEVATION WORK?

One possible explanation is simply that people like recognition. This recognition is customarily offered by those who appreciate what the person with higher status has accomplished. But what happens if few people understand why a person deserves the recognition and status they are afforded? That could create problems.

David Sklansky, a renowned mathematical genius who is known for trying to figure out human behavior, has a well-thought-out answer to how individuals might go about creating elevated status in the eyes of individuals who might otherwise not afford them such recognition.

In Sklansky's words, "My lady friend . . . recently took up a new hobby, figure skating. She plunged headlong into it and used the Internet to seek out other figure skaters. She found quite a few, and many of them were very good. They weren't champions or Olympic hopefuls but had competed successfully in regional events. Even though they were experts and my friend was a beginner, they bent over backwards to encourage and teach her.

"She said they were much nicer and friendlier than the people with whom she shared previous hobbies. That surprised me, because experts at anything are usually not that friendly to beginners. Rather than just wonder, I tried to figure out what was going on.

"I concluded that one reason for their friendliness was that, despite their expertise, they were relatively obscure. Because it looks simple on television, and they were not world-class skaters, relatively few people could appreciate their talent and hard work. Other people didn't understand the intricacies well enough to appreciate how good they were.

"I believe that these expert skaters were so encouraging and helpful mainly because they wanted my friend to gain enough knowledge and experience to fully appreciate how good they were. I'm not saying that this motive was conscious, or that they did not also have other motives. But people who are very good at something want other people to appreciate their skills, and it usually doesn't happen. For most endeavors, the only people who appreciate your expertise are at least mildly competent at whatever you do.

"Don't get me wrong. I don't mean to say these figure skaters . . . are not nice people. I just believe that experts, but not world-class ones, have a subconscious desire to nurture beginners so they will appreciate the experts' talents."

I think you can use Sklansky's insight to your benefit. If you want to develop your skills, particularly relatively rare ones, you may get some free advice and maybe even free lessons from experts or near experts. Look for someone who is good but not famous and then butter him up and ask for help. Putting it on a little thicker than you actually feel can't hurt.

In sum, using status elevation, demotion, and recognition will help you elicit information that is most likely truthful because the person does not see it as manipulation and his or her defenses are not aroused. To be effective, the status and/or recognition should be *deserved* and not manufactured in an attempt to influence the person of interest to give up information you are seeking. If a person senses you are not being sincere in affording him or her status and/or recognition, they will more than likely distrust and dislike you for your deception and will match yours with their own. Not a good recipe for becoming an effective truth detector!

CHAPTER 10

Empathetic Statements

Courage is what it takes to stand up and speak;
courage is also what it takes to sit down and listen.
WINSTON CHURCHILL

The empathetic statement is a powerful elicitation tool. Empathetic statements differ from presumptive statements in that presumptive statements are either true or false. Empathetic statements identify the physical or mental state of the elicitation target or what the elicitation target said and, using parallel language, mirrors back to the elicitation target what he or she feels or just said. Empathetic statements send the message *I am listening to you.* Changing the focus of a conversation from you to your elicitation target requires empathy. Empathy is the ability to look at life through the eyes of your elicitation target.

We have already discussed the importance of empathy and empathetic statements in Chapter 3. There I showed you how doctors can more effectively get truthful information from their patients by using empathetic statements. Patients willingly provide additional information when they know someone is listening. To increase information yield, I suggested that physicians nod and use verbal encouragement such as "I see," "Go on," and "Okay" to sustain patient commentary. The use of nodding and encouragement signals approval and continued attention and promotes discourse. Frequent nodding during conversations also increases the amount of speech by a factor of three or four.

The effective use of empathetic statements to elicit truthful information is certainly not limited to health care. Using empathetic statements can also help you learn the truth from your kids, friends, significant others, and even strangers whom you might interact with in the course of your daily activities.

In this chapter I thought it might be interesting to give you a few more examples of how salespeople and doctors use empathetic statements to enhance their service and effectiveness and do so in the most efficient manner possible. The empathetic statement is not only a good elicitation tool; empathetic statements also serve as a good rapport-building tool.

As a reminder, the basic formula for constructing empathetic statements directed at your customer is "So you . . ." This simple construction lets customers know you are really listening to them. Simple empathetic statements might include "So you like the way things are going today . . ." or "So you're having a good day . . ." The basic "So you . . ." formula ensures that the focus of the conversation remains on the customer. The empathetic statement presents a fact but leaves the interpretation of that fact to the customer. If the statement is true, the customer will usually add new information that can be helpful. If the salesperson's empathetic statement is false, the customer will typically correct it.

DISCOVERING WHAT CUSTOMERS WANT

In typical sales situations, short-term rapport-building skills are required to let the customer know the salesperson is not a threat. Potential consumers typically have their defenses up because they view salespeople as trying to take advantage of them. The goal of the salesperson, then, is to establish rapport with the customer, so they lower their guard and allow the salesperson into their personal and psychological space. The short-term rapport-building skills discussed in Chapter 3 can achieve this goal in a matter of seconds.

Once the threat level for the customer has been reduced through the "big three" friendship signals, the salesperson can then use the empathetic statement elicitation approach to solidify the rapport and glean additional information from the customer about what they are seeking to purchase. Empathetic statements keep the focus of the conversation on the customer and make them feel good about themselves. We like others who are interested in what we say and how we feel. When we say something, we want feedback to know if our message was received and understood. Good elicitors let customers know their communication was heard and understood. However, be mindful not to repeat back word for word what a person says, because parroting sounds patronizing and condescending. Consider the following example:

SALESPERSON: May I help you?

CUSTOMER: Yes. I have to buy a new washer and dryer.

SALESPERSON: So your old washer and dryer are on their last legs. [Empathetic statement.]

CUSTOMER: No, I'm moving to a small apartment.
[Correcting the initial empathetic statement.]

SALESPERSON: Oh, you need to downsize. [Empathetic statement.] Let me show you a popular stacked unit that we sell. It was designed to save you space.

CUSTOMER: Okay.

The salesperson used the empathetic statement to keep the focus on the customer and to encourage him to affirm or deny its validity: "So your old washer and dryer are on their last legs." The customer corrected the salesperson by saying, "I'm moving to a small apartment." This additional information identified what type of unit the salesperson needed to focus on selling. The words "have to buy" indicate that the customer was serious about purchasing a washing machine and dryer as opposed to just "shopping around." "Have to buy" also indicates the customer has an immediate need and is under some pressure to acquire the item under consideration.

The salesperson obtained important information during this brief conversational exchange. First, the customer is a serious buyer, and, second, the salesperson knows exactly what category of washer and dryer the customer is likely to purchase. This information saves the customer and the salesperson time. The customer goes home with the product he or she wants, and the salesperson has more time to serve other customers.

Using empathetic statements creates a win-win situation. As the salesperson you make the sale, and as the customer you get to buy the right product as quickly as possible. This creates goodwill and repeat business.

GIVING THEM A DOSE OF THEIR OWN MEDICINE

When I visited my doctor for my annual physical exam, we got to talking about the new book I was writing (this one). He asked me about the subject matter, and I briefly explained it was about elicitation and what it could accomplish. My doctor thought for a few moments and then said he had an example of elicitation I could use in the book. It turns out that my doctor performs certain procedures that require his patients to have not missed a dose of blood-thinning medicine. If a patient misses a dose, the procedure cannot be performed.

The doctor went on to explain that he used to ask his patients if they missed a dose of their medicine. Their answer was inevitably "No, I didn't miss a dose." The doctor suspected that his patients were not always telling the truth. Instead of asking directly "Did you miss a dose of your medicine?" he tried elicitation. He began with an empathetic statement, "You're a busy person," followed by a presumptive statement, "Forgetting to take your medicine every day is normal." He followed this comment up with a second empathetic statement, "It happens all the time."

My doctor told me that these linked elicitation techniques typically produced honest responses from his patients. He noted that elicitation techniques are less threatening than direct questions and provided him with a powerful tool to get at the truth. He added he had told several of his colleagues of the success he had achieved with his new approach, and they intended to adopt it with their patients as well.

In another example, a doctor felt she wasn't getting full disclosure from her patient concerning his medical conditions, so she started her medical history inquiry by using empathetic statements, which sent the message *I am hearing what you are saying.* As the patient relaxed, he began to willingly provide additional information when he realized someone was actually *listening* to him. To encourage the patient to supply more information, the doctor would nod her head and use verbal encouragers such as "I see," "Go on," and "Okay," to keep him talking. The doctor didn't simply record the patient's complaints; she used empathetic statements to encourage him to talk further about them. The following represents a typical exchange between the doctor and a patient.

> PATIENT: Lately I've had a hard time sleeping at night.
>
> DOCTOR: So you can't get to sleep. [Basic empathetic statement.]

The empathetic statement not only tells the patient *I am listening to you* but also encourages the patient to provide additional information. If patients think their doctors listen to them, the likelihood that they will provide additional information significantly increases, as seen in the following exchange:

> PATIENT: I've been having trouble with indigestion lately.
>
> DOCTOR: So you're having some stomach trouble. [Basic empathetic statement.]
>
> PATIENT: I lie awake and worry about losing my job at the plant. I can't help it. Things are really slowing down and layoffs are bound to come. My stomach is tied up in knots.

The doctor's empathetic statement encouraged the patient to provide a specific reason why he was having gastric problems.

This in turn gave the doctor a better handle on what was causing the problem so she could choose the most appropriate treatment option.

The empathetic statement is another valuable elicitation technique at your disposal. Used alone or in conjunction with other techniques, it can be a powerful truth detector while at the same time offering you collateral benefits such as increased business success, better health care, and better personal relationships.

CHAPTER 11

Naïveté

I really believe in completely being naïve and having
high hopes when meeting someone new.

FIONA APPLE

Detective/crime shows have been a staple of American television for generations of enthusiastic viewers. One of the most popular examples of the genre was *Columbo*, featuring a detective who, in his wrinkled raincoat and with his bumbling, easygoing style, came across as a friendly fellow who didn't have the smarts to do much serious crime solving. It was all a façade. Columbo was a skilled elicitor with a keen mind who used his country bumpkin image to lull adversaries into a sense of false security.

One of the techniques Columbo used effectively to elicit the truth from suspected criminals was naïveté. In fact, in their book *Mediation Theory and Practice*, authors Suzanne McCorkle and Melanie J. Reese refer to Columbo as "the naïve detective." Naïveté doesn't mean pretending you're stupid. Even the smartest people have gaps in knowledge. No one can know everything. Naïveté is effective when the technique is combined with a sincere dose of curiosity.

Displaying naïveté is an excellent way to get people talking while cloaking your true intentions. For several of the reasons discussed in Chapter 3, individuals are predisposed to talk when conversing with someone they perceive is naïve. When I use naïveté as an elicitation tool, I am amazed at what people say with very little prodding—truthful information that could have serious consequences for the speaker. This technique is also useful when you don't have sufficient information to make empathetic statements or form presumptive questions while trying to fake being an expert.

MURDER, HE SPOKE

In Chapter 9, I discussed status elevation and how I used it to gain information from members of a gang who were committing hate crimes in California. One thing you will discover as you practice elicitation and get more comfortable using it is that often using more than one elicitation technique, or even several in combination, can produce even better results in obtaining truthful information and more of it. This was the case with the skinhead gang. The most important information I gained from my elicitation of gang members came directly from using the naïve elicitation technique.

On my first visit to the skinheads' run-down house near downtown Lancaster, my goal was to find out who they were, what they believed, and any information that would relate to the crimes they were suspected of committing. As six of them gathered on the porch and spoke with me about their white supremacist ideology, I noticed that they were covered with tattoos. I was curious as to what each tattoo meant. In this case

I didn't have to feign naïveté, as many of the markings were unknown to me.

I turned to one of the gang members, pointed to a large swastika on his chest, and asked him what the tattoo meant. He told me it represented the Nazi ideology of the supremacy of the white race. I nodded and asked him about a set of 8s tattooed on his stomach. He explained that *H* is the eighth letter in the alphabet. The two eights represented "HH," short for "Heil Hitler." He volunteered that tattoos with 420 represented April 20, Hitler's birthday.

Turning to another skinhead, I pointed to a set of lightning bolts tattooed on his arm. The skinhead told me that the lightning bolts were worn by Nazi SS troopers. He then proudly revealed that members of the gang could earn the right to get lightning bolts tattooed on the inside of their biceps only when they killed someone from a hated minority group, in this case a black person.

Wow! I couldn't believe what I had just heard. This skinhead had just admitted to murder.

I also realized that the skinhead didn't realize he had just confessed to a capital offense. To avoid alerting him to his admission, I continued to ask about other tattoos. After learning the meaning of those markings, I thanked them for speaking with me, warned them to stay out of trouble, and said goodbye.

Of course, that wasn't the end of it. I got lucky. One of the skinheads I had spoken with several times turned out to be guilty of stabbing the African American student with a screwdriver on the Antelope Valley High School campus. He was sentenced to twelve years in prison for his involvement in the crime.

Approximately four months into his sentence, he called me and said he had something "really important" to tell me. I went to the prison and spoke with him. The first thing I said was "I know why you called me. You're going to give me some information, probably false, to try and get your sentence reduced."

He answered, "No, I've found religion in jail and feel I need to confess something."

If he was telling me the truth, I now knew his motive for calling me. But I still wanted to know why he chose me, considering that I had been instrumental in getting him convicted. He told me I was the only person who had treated him with respect. "I knew you were there to try and put me in jail, but you did it respectfully" was the way he put it. He then revealed his information. He knew that some gang members had killed a black man. He went on to describe where and how it happened and noted that the murderer earned his lightning bolts because of it.

I asked, "Is there any chance that the guy who was on the porch that day with the bolts on his arm was involved in that murder?"

"Yes, he was there," he replied.

With that piece of information, I was able to link that gang member to the unsolved murder.

It turned out that in November 1995 four members of the Nazi Low Riders brutally beat a forty-three-year-old black homeless man in a vacant lot behind a fast-food restaurant. The skinheads struck the victim thirteen times on the head and face with a two-by-four. Immediately after the attack, the skinheads went to a tattoo artist's house, woke him up, and demanded he tattoo them on the spot because they just killed a black man and earned their bolts.

The skinheads were subsequently tried for murder. Two of them were sentenced to life without parole. Another skinhead got a nine-year prison term. The remaining skinhead received a reduced sentence in exchange for his testimony against the others involved.

Of the approximately fifty members of the NLR in Antelope Valley, thirty-nine were arrested and received various prison sentences. After the trials ended, the remaining skinheads left Antelope Valley for parts unknown, and the town of Lancaster could finally erase its moniker of "Gangcaster." Elicitation played a key role in gathering enough evidence to prosecute the gang members and make the city safer. It also demonstrated that a little naïveté can go a long way in procuring valuable, truthful information that would have not been disclosed using more traditional interrogation techniques.

A BOOK AND A BOSS

A friend and fellow professor from another department came to my office seeking advice. He had authored a textbook and wanted to use it in his classes. After placing his book order, the chair of his department (his boss) told him it was unethical for professors to use their own books as required texts in their classes. My friend intended to confront his chair and demand that he cite the university policy stating that using one's own textbook in class is not allowed. I cautioned my colleague that a confrontational approach might just escalate the situation. Instead, I advised him to use elicitation to get the information he wanted. He gave me a quizzical look.

I briefly explained what elicitation was and suggested he use naïveté to achieve his objective. I added that timing was important. "Wait for a time when your chair is not busy," I advised. "Busy people do not want to be burdened with additional things to do, especially problematic issues." I also talked with my friend about building rapport and the importance of displaying the friend signals when he entered the chair's office. "That will help send the message that the meeting is not meant to be confrontational," I explained.

"Once you sit down with your boss, ask for his advice," I continued. "Tell him that you read the university's policy regarding the use of textbooks and could not find a statement prohibiting professors from using their own textbooks in their classes. Add that you were hoping the chair could help you clarify the textbook policy."

Taking the naïve approach placed the chair in a position where he was psychologically predisposed to assist my friend. Furthermore, he now had to produce evidence of the university policy prohibiting professors from using their own books in class. If the chair was wrong or had misinterpreted the textbook policy, he could easily save face, because my friend's approach was cooperative and not adversarial. Eliciting information from the chair about the textbook policy would yield the information needed while preserving a positive relationship between my friend and his boss.

A week later my friend stopped by with a big grin on his face. He informed me that there was in fact no university policy prohibiting professors from using their own textbooks in their classes. He also told me that the elicitation approach I had showed him worked like a charm. In fact, he was going to use the same approach to solve future work problems.

CATCHING A KICKBACK

In my work with the FBI, I was assigned to a case involving possible fraud by a government official who was suspected of taking kickbacks from government contractors. It was believed the individual was getting $25,000 for awarding a contract. The kickback was rolled into the contract price, so the contractor was not out any money to get this favored treatment.

Because I was a counterintelligence agent, I knew very little about the contracting process. I received a quick overview of how the process worked from an honest government contracting officer. Armed with this minimal information, I interviewed the target of the investigation. I knew I couldn't fake a thorough knowledge of the subject. I also suspected I would not get a straight answer from him if I asked direct questions. For this interview I realized that elicitation was my best investigative tool for getting at the truth. My weapon of choice was naïveté.

I told the target up front that I was a counterintelligence agent and not well versed in contracting rules and regulations. I added that I heard he was an expert in the contracting process. I then politely asked him to explain the process to me. I knew full well that the target would tell the truth about the process. He was compelled to demonstrate the expertise I accorded him.

He explained the contracting process step by step. Along the way, he mentioned that he had received several awards for his negotiating prowess. When he finished his explanation, I sat in feigned awe. I remarked, "Wow, you sure know the contracting process inside and out. Nothing gets by you!"

"Yup," he agreed, "that's why they pay me the big bucks."

I reached into my briefcase and pulled out the suspicious

contract. I placed it on the target's desk. As I pushed the document toward him, I said, "Why didn't you follow the rules with this contract?"

The target paused. The gotcha moment passed. The target said as calmly as he could, "That contract is different."

"Yeah," I replied. "You took a $25,000 kickback for this contract."

Using elicitation, I was able to get the target to tell me the truth. After he had explained the contracting process in elaborate detail, he couldn't claim that he didn't know what he was doing or pass the error off as an oversight.

The moral of the story? In many cases it is better to elicit the truth rather than confront deception directly by making accusations.

NAÏVETÉ VERSUS HUMAN NATURE

Acting naïve to gain truthful information is an effective elicitation tool, but it comes with a cost. That cost involves *ego suspension*, a topic discussed earlier in the book. When you act naïve, you are basically putting yourself in an inferior position to your person of interest; after all, by using the technique, you're basically saying you aren't as smart or knowledgeable or informed as someone else. Sometimes that may be true and sometimes it may not be; regardless, it goes against basic human nature to purposely and knowingly place yourself in an inferior position to someone else.

That doesn't mean you shouldn't do it! Remember that the ability to suppress one's ego is a vital attribute for any good truth detector. When using naïveté as an elicitation technique, think of Detective Columbo and view yourself as an actor playing a role to gain your objective. The role is *not you*. And your focus should be on the person of interest, *not yourself*. Once you think of naïveté in these terms, I believe you will be able to use the technique in a believable manner to great benefit: the acquisition of information you might not get otherwise.

ELICITING FROM PEOPLE IN AUTHORITY

Eliciting information from people in authority can be a bit tricky and requires some planning, because you don't want to alienate them by raising yourself to their level. First, you will want to say something that will allow them to flatter themselves. This helps to establish rapport or to reinforce rapport that has already been established. In this case the elicitation tool of choice is naïveté. People in authority naturally think they know more than their subordinates. People in authority also tend to reveal more information than required in order to demonstrate that they do, in fact, know more than their subordinates. A display of naïveté reaffirms the supervisor-subordinate relationship.

Along with naïveté, you can use the presumptive statement in the form of a true-or-false assertion. The presumptive statement is a natural companion of naïveté because naïve people are not expected to know the ins and outs of a topic. Naiveté permits the elicitor to speculate and make assertions that a more knowledgeable person would not make. The combination of naïveté and the presumptive statement taps into the human tendency for people to correct others and demonstrate expertise.

People in authority are inclined to dominate conversations. This tendency can be exploited by introducing empathetic statements into a conversation. Mirroring back what the person in authority said lets that person know you are listening to him or her. Empathetic statements encourage additional conversation. The more people talk, the more information they reveal. So the best approach to elicit information from people in authority is to daisy-chain naïveté, empathetic statements, and presumptive statements. This combination of elicitation approaches allows the person of authority to maintain their sense of higher status, makes them feel good about themselves, and allows them to show off their expertise.

CHAPTER 12

Some Additional Techniques to Place in Your Elicitation Toolbox

Truth may not always be confessed
MUNIA KHAN

I've included some additional elicitation tools in this chapter that you might find useful in your role as a truth detector. That these tools don't have their own designated chapter in no way minimizes their effectiveness or usefulness in eliciting information from persons of interest. In fact, depending on your preferences and experiences with the various elicitation techniques, you may find some of the ones included in this chapter to be among your favorite, most frequently used approaches when eliciting information.

QUOTATION OF REPORTED FACTS

There is power in the words "I saw it on the Internet," "I read it in the newspaper," and "I saw it on the TV news." An elicitor can use those words to get information from persons of interest. How? By constructing a statement, either true or false, that he or she claimed to have heard from a media source (a newspaper, a magazine, a blog, TV news, etc.) that is relevant to the information being elicited.

For example, let's assume that you work in manufacturing and want to know if your competitor is having difficulty filling orders due to problems on their assembly line. You the elicitor could approach your rival salesperson and state, "I read on the Internet that your company is having trouble meeting your delivery deadlines because of production problems." The target of the elicitation will either confirm or deny the report based on the human need to correct others. Additionally, the elicitation target will rationalize that if the information is already out there, what's the harm in talking about it?

Here is an example of the "reported-facts" approach in a business setting. Tim owns stock in Company A. Tim wants to know if the quarterly earnings might affect the price of the stock. If the quarterly earnings are down, Tim wants to sell short to avoid a loss. If the quarterly earnings are good, then Tim wants to buy more stock in Company A before the stock price goes up. Tim's neighbor is employed by Company A. The following conversation between Tim and his neighbor illustrates the use of reported facts.

TIM: I was looking at the Internet and read that some analysts expect your company's quarterly earnings to be off by 15 percent due to the tariff issues with China.

NEIGHBOR: Well, as usual, the media has it all wrong. In fact, the company is making plans to bring

manufacturing back to the United States. That should
help the bottom line quite a bit.

Having procured the information he sought, Tim crafts a response designed to deflect the real reason for his inquiry:

TIM: I should have known better than to believe everything
I read on the Internet.

CREATING COGNITIVE DISSONANCE TO ELICIT THE TRUTH

As I pointed out in Chapter 3, cognitive dissonance occurs when
a person holds two opposing ideas simultaneously. Cognitive
dissonance can also occur when people are presented with ideas
that are in direct opposition to what they think or believe. This
causes feelings of discomfort and anxiety. The greater the cognitive dissonance, the more pressure a person feels to alleviate the
anxiety. Elicitors gain valuable information when they can create
cognitive dissonance in a person of interest, who is more likely to
divulge truthful information without realizing it while in a state
of mental conflict.

Inducing cognitive dissonance proved a successful technique
when interviewing Islamic terrorists. An Army interrogator was
interrogating a particularly difficult terrorist who did not want
to confess to setting off a bomb in a crowded marketplace. I was
asked to review the case and make suggestions. I instructed the
interviewer to ask the terrorist what it meant to be a good Muslim. The terrorist recited the five pillars of Islam: faith, prayer,
charity, fasting, and a pilgrimage to Mecca. To my surprise, the

terrorist added, "And not hurt innocent Muslims, especially women and children."

After the terrorist established his own baseline of what he thought a good Muslim should be, the interviewer induced cognitive dissonance. He did so by methodically reviewing the damage caused by the remote bomb. The interviewer emphasized that many Muslim women and children had been killed or hurt as a result of the bomb.

The terrorist had three choices. First, he could admit that, by his own definition, he was not a good Muslim. Second, he could try to rationalize his actions to prove to the interrogator that he was a good Muslim despite the fact that Muslim women and children had been injured and killed. Third, he could outright dismiss the inference that he was not a good Muslim. The terrorist chose to justify to the interviewer that he was a good Muslim. During the terrorist's rationalization process, he admitted to planting the bomb and setting it off.

David Sklansky speaks to the issue of what happens when you create cognitive dissonance in an individual. The result is a mental disequilibrium so overwhelming that the person of interest reveals not only critical, true information but, amazingly, information they had not mentally accepted until that moment as real.

Sklansky relates the story of one such case of induced cognitive dissonance. "Many years ago, a girl I really cared about started drinking too much. Before we met she had a drinking problem but seemed to have it under control when we were together. After not seeing each other for a while, it looked like the problem was back. She claimed it wasn't. She admitted that she liked to drink but said that her drinking was totally under her control. She could take it or leave it. This woman had very little money. I decided to test her drinking claim and asked her, 'If I offered to give you a hundred dollars a day if you don't drink, would you take it?'

"Thinking I wasn't serious, she quickly replied, 'Of course. I'd love that deal.'

" 'Okay. You've got it,' I said.

"She immediately started crying. When I asked why, she said, 'I never thought you would actually do that. But I believe you, and it's a deal, and the money will be great. I cried because the moment you offered to pay me, my first reaction was dread, not happiness. You made me realize I actually am an alcoholic.'

"She stayed on the wagon for only two weeks."

QUID PRO QUO: MAKING AN INFORMATION DEAL

Quid pro quo is an elicitation technique that encourages people to match information provided by others. For example, you meet a person for the first time and want to know where they work. Instead of directly asking that individual "Where do you work?," tell them where you work first. People will tend to reciprocate (see Chapter 3) by telling you where *they* work. This elicitation technique can be used to discover information about people without being intrusive and appearing nosy.

If you don't want people to know where you work, you can get the needed information from the other person and short-circuit the reciprocity by asking the question in a novel way. The typical exchange is "Where do you work?" The other person replies and then reciprocates with "Where do *you* work?" To short-circuit reciprocity in this case, ask the question in a novel way. Ask, "Where do you labor?" This question requires additional cognitive processing, which disrupts the need to reciprocate with "Where do you work?"

Student loans can place a hardship on long-term relationships. Paying back these loans can forestall marriage, having children, and buying a house. Directly asking a person you want to get into a serious relationship with about the amount of student loan debt they have is impolite and may provoke a dishonest response. Realistically, such a question could kill a fledgling relationship. The quid pro quo elicitation technique is a better way to obtain this sensitive information while not appearing nosy or rude. Such a conversation might go down in the following manner:

> YOU: I'm going to have to order a light meal, because I'm watching my budget this month. I have my student loan due in less than a week, and it's several hundred dollars a month.
>
> ROMANTIC INTEREST: I know what you mean. My student loan is $900 a month.
>
> YOU: Wow, I thought mine was a lot. You must be paying yours off faster.
>
> ROMANTIC INTEREST: I still have eight years left.
>
> YOU: I think I'll order a Cobb salad.
>
> ROMANTIC INTEREST: I'm going to go with the spaghetti.

Your romantic interest revealed sensitive information about their financial situation. Now you have the information you need to decide if you want to get into a long-term relationship or not.

IF AT FIRST YOU DON'T SUCCEED, TRY, TRY A FRIEND...

There will be times when your elicitation efforts fail to get the information you need. Maybe your targeted subject doesn't know the data in the first place. Or possibly they are so secretive that no amount of effort on your part will pry the coveted knowledge from between their compressed lips. There is also the chance you might have aroused suspicion in your person of interest because you made an error in your approach. Hey, even the best elicitors can make mistakes and blow an elicitation attempt!

Does that doom you to failure? Not necessarily. In many instances, particularly when dealing with situations in which more than one person might be able to provide you with the information you seek, you always have the option of approaching someone else to see if you can extract the information from them. Here is a classic example of how I used this tactic to turn a first-elicitation failure into a second-elicitation success.

I had heard rumors that Company A was going to move their operations from our city to a city in a southern state to save money in taxes and labor costs. If the rumor was true, it would affect not only myself but several of my friends who stood to lose a lot of money on real estate.

My neighbor, Philip, was employed by Company A. I was not sure what position he held in the organization but thought it was worth a shot to try to elicit information from him about the possible relocation. Several weeks later my wife and I were invited to a party given by a friend. Coincidentally, Philip and his wife were invited to the same party. At one point during the festivities, I approached Philip and engaged in some neighborhood small talk. After a few minutes I casually said, "I heard rumors to the effect that your company is going to relocate out of state." Without hesitation Philip told me that those rumors had been circulating for years and had no basis in fact. I tried several more times without success to draw out information about the rumors. I closed our conversation with a few more minutes of neighborhood chitchat and moved on.

Not to be discouraged, I decided to take another approach. If Philip wasn't willing to talk, perhaps his wife would. I mingled with the other guests until I had an opportunity to talk to her. Philip's wife was more outgoing and sociable than her husband. I engaged her in some small talk about the weather. I pivoted the conversation to the incredibly harsh winter we had experienced the year before. She agreed with my assessment of the winter. She then added that she hated the cold weather and was glad she wouldn't have to worry about that next year. When I nodded, she exclaimed that she was thankful to be moving to a southern state where it would be warmer. Upon hearing this, I changed the subject by asking her how her garden was doing. She became very excited, told me it was flourishing, and offered to give me some of her harvest in the fall. After "harvesting" the information I needed, I was tempted to mention that her offer would mean a second harvest, but of course I didn't! I graciously accepted her gift and moved on. By allowing Philip's wife to complain about the cold weather, I was able to obtain the valuable information about the company's investment that I sought.

BEING A SKEPTIC: THE "DOUBTING THOMAS" TECHNIQUE

When people are exposed to skepticism, they believe that their statements lack credibility and they feel the need to provide additional information to convince the listener that what they are saying is truthful. This added information often contains sensitive information. The following example describes how a father used the skepticism technique to learn the truth about his son's performance in school.

DAD: How are your grades coming along?

SON: Good. I'm really doing well this semester.

DAD: Really well, huh? [Voice slightly rising, indicating his skepticism.]

SON: Well, most of my classes, anyway.

DAD: Let's talk about the classes you're not doing well in.

SON: Math is really hard. We're studying algebra.

DAD: I'm pretty good at algebra. How about if we spend an hour or so going over your homework every night?

SON: Cool. Thanks.

I often used skepticism in my law enforcement career. On one occasion I was interviewing a burglar who knocked a hole in a wall to enter an optician's office to circumvent the alarm system. Once in the store, the burglar stole $30,000 worth of designer eye-glass frames, maintaining that he was the only person to knock the hole in the brick wall. The following interview excerpt demonstrates how skepticism elicited additional important information.

> **ME:** That hole in the wall must've taken several people to knock out.
>
> **BURGLAR:** Nope. Just me.
>
> **ME:** Come on. You couldn't have done it alone. It took more than one guy just to haul the tools into the store. [Skepticism.]
>
> **BURGLAR:** The tools aren't heavy. We each carried some and made it in one trip.
>
> **ME:** Did you hear what you just said?
>
> **BURGLAR:** Huh?
>
> **ME:** You said, "We each carried some . . ." That means you had help.
>
> **BURGLAR:** Oh . . .
>
> **ME:** Talk to me.
>
> **BURGLAR:** My brother and his friend were there.

MIXING SKEPTICISM WITH A PRESUMPTIVE STATEMENT AND A DASH OF QUOTATION OF REPORTED FACTS

My wife and I went away for a weekend vacation. We believed our high school–age teens were old enough and responsible enough to be left alone for a few days. However, we did have lingering doubts. Upon our return, the house was spotlessly clean. This was our first clue that something had happened while we were away. The house is never that clean even when we prod the kids to straighten up their rooms or do other household chores.

That night at dinner, I casually mentioned that we talked to one of the neighbors, who told us that a party got out of control and the police were called (quotation of reported facts).

My oldest daughter spontaneously replied, "The police didn't come."

I countered with "So the party did not get out of hand" (presumptive statement).

My daughter suddenly realized she had admitted that there had in fact been a party. She stammered for a few seconds, then said, "We had a few friends over."

I gave her a quizzical look and said, "Really? *A few* friends?" (skepticism).

My daughter explained that a bunch of people just randomly showed up.

I observed, "It must have been a big party for the house to be so messy that you had to do so much cleaning. I haven't seen the house this clean since I don't know when" (presumptive statement).

"Yeah," my daughter finally admitted, "it was a big party."

My wife and I were disappointed with our daughter's decision to throw a party in our absence. It took a while before she regained our trust.

A few days later I told a colleague at work about our daughter's party and how I had elicited the truth from her even though I did not know for sure whether she had thrown a party. My colleague chuckled and told me that he had had a similar experience. He noted that he instinctively used a similar elicitation technique but did not know that what he had done had a formal name.

He, too, suspected that his son had thrown a party in his

absence. When he arrived home, the house was clean. However, when he walked through the living room, he noticed that the carpet had a sticky spot. My colleague backed up and stepped on the sticky spot again. He told me his son grimaced and looked worried. My colleague stepped on the sticky spot yet again and said, "Someone spilled a drink here. It must have been a wild party you threw" (presumptive statement). His son immediately confessed that he had invited a few friends over and the party got out of control. My colleague said he was glad that we talked because now he had a name for what he had done.

FEIGNED DISBELIEF

A mere expression of disbelief will often result in further enlightenment when it comes to eliciting the truth. Statements such as "You're kidding! Really?" or "That can't be true" puts the targeted subject in a position of defending his or her statement. In doing so, information of value can be revealed. Here's an example most poker players will appreciate:

> HUSBAND: Guess what, honey, I won $3,000 at the tournament tonight!
>
> WIFE: Really? That's hard to imagine! [Feigned disbelief.]
>
> HUSBAND: I know it sounds crazy, but I couldn't lose a hand.
>
> WIFE: You said you felt unlucky before you left. I don't see how you won. [Feigned disbelief.]
>
> HUSBAND: That's poker. I was on a heater. Had pocket aces three times.

WIFE: *Three times?* That's unbelievable! [Feigned disbelief.]

HUSBAND: Well, it happened, and they held up each time.

WIFE: I'd be surprised if I went on the Hendon Mob poker website and saw you up $3,000 on your total winnings.[Feigned disbelief. The Hendon Mob tracks money won by poker players around the world.]

HUSBAND: [Flustered.] Well, I *would* have won if a donkey hadn't called my pocket aces with a 4–6 offsuit and hit a straight.

WORD ECHO: EXTENDING THE ELICITATION ENCOUNTER

The word echo technique is used during elicitations to encourage the targeted individual to keep speaking and provide additional information to you, the listener. This is accomplished by basically repeating the last word or two of what the person of interest last said if he or she pauses and needs some encouragement to continue. During the following conversation, a headhunter is speaking with an employee of a company to look for a way to entice fellow employees to jump ship for new employment opportunities. If the employees are not happy, they are more likely to want to look for new positions.

EMPLOYEE: Working here is not easy.

HEADHUNTER: That must present a challenge. [Presumptive statement.]

EMPLOYEE: They treat their staff unfairly.

HEADHUNTER: Unfairly. [Word echo.]

EMPLOYEE: Exactly. They don't pay us for the work we do.

HEADHUNTER: That must really bother you. [Presumptive statement.]

EMPLOYEE: It does. And it keeps getting worse.

HEADHUNTER: Things don't seem to be getting better. [Empathetic statement.]

EMPLOYEE: It all started when they hired a new CFO [chief financial officer]. The guy is a real bean counter. Saving money at our expense.

HEADHUNTER: Sounds really bad. [Empathetic statement.]

EMPLOYEE: You wouldn't believe it. We're supposed to get an hour for lunch, but we rarely get half that time. We're shorted on our breaks too. And overtime is the worst. We're supposed to get time and a half, but we usually end up with no extra pay. It's so bad we call it "outa pocket overtime."

HEADHUNTER: "Outa pocket overtime." [Word echo.]

EMPLOYEE: It makes it pretty hard to get up and go to work every day.

This is only one employee expressing his opinion; however, he complained about a systemic problem at his company, which suggests that other employees likely feel the same way. Armed with this information, the headhunter can now develop a recruitment strategy that will directly appeal to the disgruntled employees at that company.

ERRONEOUS MISATTRIBUTION

Erroneous misattribution occurs when the elicitor attributes skills not readily associated with the person they are describing. For example, the elicitor casually mentions to the elicitation target that an old person should know how to use Instagram, Snapchat, or some other social media platforms associated with young people. The elicitation target will often correct the elicitor. During the process of making the correction, the elicitation target reveals information that they would not normally provide during a conversation with a stranger.

HANGING CHAD

People often start sentences and, for various reasons, stop in mid-sentence. They stop speaking for a reason. If you want to know the reason, you can repeat the hanging portion of the conversation (word echo) and wait for a response. The hanging chad technique allows the target to finish the sentence or idea presented by the elicitor.

The hanging chad technique works best on extroverted elicitation targets because extroverts readily complete people's sentences. I often used this technique when meeting interviewees for the first time. I would say something to the effect of "I'm trying to think of the name of your best friend. His name is . . . ah . . ." An extroverted interviewee would spontaneously fill in the name, giving me information I didn't know before. Best friends tend to reveal sensitive information to one another. Knowing who the interviewee's best friend is gave me a potentially valuable lead in either verifying or disproving what the interviewee told me.

TEST-DRIVE YOUR ELICITATION TECHNIQUES

The next time you're out and about running errands, take a minute or two to practice your elicitation skills. Almost any interaction with people can be turned into an elicitation practice exercise. Start out by eliciting small bits of sensitive information such as date of birth. During the normal course of a conversation, casually pivot the conversation to age. After making the initial pivot, introduce an elicitation tool. Follow through with additional elicitation tools until you obtain the person's birth date. If for some reason you sense that the person will not reveal his or her date of birth, cease the elicitation and close the conversation with small talk. The beauty of elicitation is that your elicitation subject will not know that they were the target of your elicitation attempt.

When you first start to practice, pick people who are in a position to have to talk to you, such as salespeople in stores. This will give you the highest probability of success. Jewelry stores are a good place to obtain dates of birth. Every month has a birthstone, which can be used to pivot the conversation to the birth month of the salesperson. Consider the following elicitation approach:

> YOU: I'm looking for a present for my girlfriend. [Small
>   talk.]
>
> SALESPERSON: Do you have anything in mind
>   specifically?

YOU: I'd like to get her something with her birthstone. She was born in April. I have no idea what the birthstone is. [Pivot.]

SALESPERSON: April is diamond.

YOU: You knew that right away. You must have an April birthday too. [Presumptive statement.]

SALESPERSON: No, I was born in March.

YOU: Wow, I was born in March too. March 20. [Quid pro quo.]

SALESPERSON: My birthday is the third.

YOU: You're a lot younger than I am. You must be twenty-one to twenty-four years old. [Bracketing.]

SALESPERSON: I'm twenty-two.

YOU: I just met my girlfriend a few months ago. I don't think I'm ready to buy her a diamond yet. I'll have to think of another present. Thanks for your time. [Small talk.]

SALESPERSON: Have a nice day.

That was easy. With a little math, you obtained the salesperson's date of birth in less than three minutes, and the salesperson didn't realize that she revealed sensitive information that could be used to steal her identity.

The next time you're waiting in line to pay for something, try eliciting the date of a wedding anniversary from the customer in front of you. This is a challenge, because you have only a few minutes to obtain the information before it's your target's turn to check out. The best way to initiate a conversation is to scan the items in your target's basket. I remember the first time I tried to elicit information from someone in a grocery line. I selected an elicitation target, and I looked in her basket and saw three sizes of disposal diapers, which meant the woman had three young children. Having had children myself, I knew firsthand how hard it is to raise three young ones together. I used the common ground I shared with the woman to initiate the conversation, which went like this:

ME: Your kids must keep you very busy. [Pointing to the packages of Pampers.]

WOMAN: Yeah, they sure do.

ME: You don't look old enough to have three kids. [Pivot.] You must have gotten married when you were nineteen. [Presumptive statement.]

WOMAN: Thanks, but not quite. I was twenty-three when I got married.

ME: A June bride, no doubt. It seems like most people get married in June. [Presumptive statement.]

WOMAN: No, I got married in February.

ME: On Valentine's Day, no doubt. [Presumptive statement.]

WOMAN: No, February tenth.

This elicitation took less than a minute. The more you practice elicitation, the more sophisticated your elicitation approaches will be, and the better truth detector you will become. After a few elicitation successes, you will gain confidence in the power of the elicitation tools presented in this book. You will also discover which elicitation tools you are most comfortable using.

Becoming a good truth detector is easier than you think.

• • •

Your elicitation toolbox is now complete. You now have a full range of elicitation tools at your disposal. Practice using one or two elicitation tools you think fit your personality. Once you become proficient with them, practice using several additional elicitation tools. Continue introducing additional elicitation tools into your repertoire until you are at least comfortable using all the tools. You will soon learn which elicitation tools work best for you and in what circumstances they can be successfully applied. The only thing left for you is to become an efficient truth detector in practice. The next chapters will provide you with personality types to tailor your elicitations around and exercises you can do to hone your newly acquired skills.

CHAPTER 13

The P (Personality) Factor in Effective Elicitation

*Tell me what you pay attention to and
I will tell you who you are.*

JOSÉ ORTEGA Y GASSET

P stands for "personality." It would take an entire book, maybe more than one, to fully explain the various types of personalities people have and how the "P factor" impacts the way individuals perceive and behave in their everyday life. But one thing is certain: the more you understand about an individual's personality, the better your chances for conducting a successful elicitation.

Let me illustrate the impact and importance of the personality factor in determining human behavior and how to deal with it successfully during an elicitation. I'll describe each personality type, and then I'll show you how to use that information to conduct a more successful elicitation.

As a behavioral analyst for the FBI's National Security Division, I was often asked to assess targets for their susceptibility to being recruited as spies for the United States. This task was made more difficult because, for obvious reasons, I could not talk directly to the recruitment targets to obtain the necessary personal information needed to assess their personalities. I had to rely on remote profiling to perform personality assessments. Remote profiling is when you observe people from a distance without them knowing that they are being observed. Based on the target's behaviors, I was able to develop very accurate personality profiles.

Knowing a person's personality type before you meet them for the first time allows you to develop custom-made communication strategies. You will know where that person gets and expends energy. You will know how that person perceives the world. You will know how to communicate with that person using their preferred communication channel, and you will know how they make decisions. Profiling a recruitment target significantly increases the probability of a successful recruitment. Remote profiling is essential not only when recruiting spies to commit espionage but also in social and business settings when you are seeking truthful information about what people think or how to best make a sale.

The Myers-Briggs Type Indicator (MBTI) is a useful tool to conduct remote profiling quickly. The MBTI was based on a theory presented by Carl Jung. Jung posited that human behavior was not random but, rather, orderly and consistent. Jung initially presented his theory in an academic journal, but few people could comprehend it. During World War II, Isabel Briggs Myers and her mother, Katharine Cook Briggs, reworked Jung's theory using language that everyday people could understand. Myers and Briggs also revised Jung's theory using up-to-date research. The end result became a testing instrument known simply as the MBTI. Hundreds of studies have tested the MBTI and have proven the instrument to be reliable. Millions of people take the MBTI each year.

The MBTI is based on four sliding scales of opposite pairs. The first pair is extraversion* (E) and introversion (I). The second pair is sensing (S) and intuition (N). The third pair is thinking (T) and feeling (F), and the fourth pair is judging (J) and perceiving (P). The MBTI does not measure IQs, traits, abilities, or character. The MBTI does identify where a person's preference lies on each sliding scale. People may display behavioral characteristics on both ends of the scale; however, they demonstrate a preference for one end of the scale or the other.

The resulting MBTI psychological type consists of four letters representing the person's preference for one end of the scale (e.g., ENTP). Sixteen psychological types can be derived from the four sliding scales. No one type is better than another type. The four-letter psychological type simply indicates which end of the sliding scale people prefer. Refer to Appendix A for a brief description of each psychological type. For the reader interested in learning more about personality, I would suggest starting with an examination of the sixteen personality types explained in the Briggs's seminal text *Gifts Differing: Understanding Personality Type*.

EXTRAVERSION AND INTROVERSION

Ask yourself, *Where do I get my energy from?* If you get your energy from interacting with other people and engaging in a variety of activities, your preference is for extraversion. If you get your energy from introspection and reflecting on your inner thoughts,

---

* The Myers & Briggs Foundation's preferred spelling.

memories, and feelings, your preference is for introversion. In the United States, it is estimated that 75 percent of the population are extroverts and 25 percent are introverts.

A Deeper Dive

Extroverts get their energy from interacting with other people. Extroverts prefer to work on multiple tasks. Extroverts are spontaneous and often talk without thinking. Extroverts speak about a variety of topics, but their conversations are typically superficial. Extroverts are driven by activity and often move from one project to the next. Extroverts talk to themselves and others when they think. What extroverts say is not always what they mean. Extroverts are comfortable allowing people to really get to know them. Extroverts have a wide range of superficial personal relationships. Extroverts tend to finish other people's sentences. Extroverts are comfortable making snap decisions.

Introverts get their energy through introspection. Introverts prefer to work on fewer projects but with greater intensity. Introverts talk about fewer topics but with more in-depth knowledge. Introverts work on projects carefully thinking about the consequences of their actions. Introverts think before they speak and mean what they say. Introverts protect their privacy until they get to know the person they are talking with. Introverts maintain fewer personal relationships, but their relationships are usually long-standing and more in-depth. Introverts do not typically make snap decisions. Introverts need time to think things through, often overnight or longer, before making any decision.

EXTROVERT OR INTROVERT: PARTY UP OR PARTY DOWN?

Extroverts feed off the energy of other people, whereas introverts find their energy sapped when around others for extended periods of time. Thus, if an extrovert and an introvert arrive at a party at the same time, the extrovert will tend to become more animated and "charged up" as the night goes on, whereas the introvert will steadily lose energy, kind of like a car battery running down because the headlights were left on when the ignition was turned off. Introverts will need to return home to "recharge" their energy with some alone time, while the extrovert will leave the party more animated than when he arrived.

SOME BASIC COMMUNICATION TACTICS TO UTILIZE IN ELICITING THE TRUTH FROM EXTROVERTS

Communicating with Extroverts

Extroverts often finish other people's sentences. You can exploit this behavioral characteristic by pausing in mid-sentence. Extroverts tend to finish other people's sentences . . . and reveal interesting information in the process. Extroverts like to talk, so let them. If there is a lull in the conversation, extroverts tend to fill the silence spontaneously. They spew out words and expect listeners to sift through the accumulation of words to find the ones that are meaningful. This behavioral characteristic leaves extroverts vulnerable to elicitation. If you dig deep enough into their word piles, you will find some golden nuggets of information.

To encourage extroverts to talk more, use "nudges." Nudges

consist of head nods and verbal encouragers such as "Uh-huh," "I see," and "Go on." Extroverts think out loud. You can watch them go through their decision-making process. Knowing how people make decisions provides clues as to what sales pitch will work best if you're selling something to extroverts. Additionally, you can guide extroverts through the decision-making process and influence the outcome. Extroverts like talking about a variety of topics, so you should have several diverse topics prepared when talking with them. Keep the conversation moving. Extroverts are spontaneous and expect immediate action. They often make decisions without thinking through the unforeseen consequences of their decisions. This includes spontaneously giving up information without realizing the consequences of what they are saying.

Being a strong extrovert myself, I am prone to making snap decisions. One time I needed a new laptop computer, so I went to the store and bought the first one that seemed acceptable. After getting the computer home, I discovered that I had purchased the wrong one. All the interfaces were wrong. I had to go back out to the store and get another one, simply because I hadn't thought through my decision before making it.

Suggested Elicitation Techniques

Presumptive
Naïveté
Hanging chad
Feigned disbelief
Curiosity

SOME BASIC COMMUNICATION TACTICS TO UTILIZE IN ELICITING THE TRUTH FROM INTROVERTS

Communicating with Introverts

Introverts think before they speak. They ask questions, then listen carefully. Introverts deal with one idea or issue at a time. Give the introvert time to reflect on what you have said. No matter how tempted you might be (particularly if you're an extrovert), don't finish an introvert's sentences! When you do, that's when introverts get short-changed in a balanced conversation, and you risk the loss of valuable information. Remember: an extrovert blurts out their thoughts and keeps on going, while the introvert seldom gets enough conversational white space to craft a reply, much less say it out loud.

An instructor who taught about personality profiling once told me, "If you're an extrovert like I am and find yourself talking with an introvert, ask a question and then stop talking for a count of three. You'll be surprised at what you will learn." Remember: introverts take a moment to process information they have received before crafting a response.

Suggested Elicitation Techniques

Quid pro quo (encouragement to match information)
Word echo (repeating the last word said)
Curiosity
Quotation of quoted facts
Status manipulation
Bracketing

I Spy with My Little "I" (Introversion)

Earlier in the book, I described how elicitation was used to catch John Charlton, an engineer at Lockheed Martin, who was trying to sell stealth technology to foreign intelligence services. What I didn't mention was how personality profiling was used to make the elicitation more effective and, in the end, led to Charlton's apprehension and conviction for espionage.

Once the FBI became suspicious of Charlton, he became the target of an undercover operation. To increase the chances of the operation's success, Charlton's personality was profiled using third-party information and remote observations.

Charlton lived at home with his mother. He had few friends in the office or in the outside world. He rarely participated in social activities at work. He preferred to sit alone at his desk, diligently working on his assigned tasks. He rarely spoke during meetings, and when he did speak, what he said was meaningful. When he did make decisions, Charlton first was careful to weigh the pros and cons of all possible options.

Putting all this information together, I surmised that Charlton was most likely an introvert. Thus, when I chose the undercover agent, I selected another introvert to contact him. People like other individuals most like themselves. I also wanted to avoid another phenomenon. When introverts meet extroverts for the first time, they are predisposed to dislike them. That is because introverts see extroverts as arrogant, obnoxious know-it-alls who are overconfident and aggressive. Conversely, when extroverts meet introverts for the first time, they are predisposed to dislike them as well. That is because they see introverts as nerdy, quiet, and not very friendly. These predispositions have nothing to do with what you say or do but rest solely on your personality.

Sending in an introvert to meet with Charlton avoided this potential game ender.

The FBI undercover agent posed as a transportation expert working for the French government, and he developed an instant rapport with Charlton. In fact, during the postarrest interview, Charlton commented several times that he liked the undercover agent because they had so many things in common. They did have a common bond: their matching introverted nature.

Whenever possible, an elicitor should find out as much as possible about a potential person of interest's personality before moving forward. Once armed with that knowledge, the elicitor should use it to customize the elicitation to gain critical information more successfully.

Many times, identifying the personality preferences making up the 16 personality MBTI types is not possible due to the lack of personal information. Identifying the personality preferences of a person when we first meet them is difficult because we don't know that person very well. The longer you know a person, the more of their personality types are revealed. Extroversion and introversion are probably the easiest aspects of personality to identify. This is because extroversion and introversion indicate the way people interact with the world around them. Simply observing people's behaviors can provide clues of extroversion or introversion. Knowing if someone is an extrovert or an introvert allows you to tailor your communication style and choose the most suitable elicitation technique. With practice, identifying extroverts and introverts will become second nature.

In the event that you are able to identify only a few MBTI personality types, I will present some basic communication tactics to utilize in each of the eight MBTI personality types and suggest elicitation techniques. The basic elicitation techniques are only recommendations based on a broad understanding of MBTI personality types. Each person is different. As always, if the recommended elicitation technique does not work, try others. No single elicitation technique works for all situations, but for all situations there is an elicitation technique that will work.

SENSING AND INTUITION

Ask yourself, *How do you prefer to take in information?* If you prefer to take in information through your five senses, are observant about specifics, and are attuned to practical realities, then your preference is for sensing. If you prefer looking at the big picture, see relationships and connections between facts, and see new possibilities, then your preference is for intuition.

A Deeper Dive
People who prefer sensing pay more attention to facts and details. Sensors see individual trees and not the forest. Sensors think in a linear fashion. Sensors like the familiar and live in the here and now with their feet planted firmly on the ground. Sensors like specific instructions when performing tasks. Sensors seek previously successful solutions to solve present problems. Sensors like to get things done using a step-by-step process. Sensors do not like to change plans in midstream. Sensors like new ideas only if the ideas have practical applications.

People who prefer intuiting look for the big picture making connections, read between the lines, and seek underlying meanings. Intuitives see the forest and not individual trees. Intuitives make leaps in their thought process and can see connections between ideas that are not obviously connected. Intuitives are often seen as having their heads in the clouds, chasing the idea fairy. Intuitives enjoy inventing things. Intuitives rely on their gut instinct when making decisions and seek novel ways to solve problems without relying on what worked in the past. Intuitives enjoy the creative process of completing tasks and solving problems.

SOME BASIC COMMUNICATION TACTICS TO UTILIZE IN ELICITING THE TRUTH FROM SENSORS

Communicating with Sensors

Sensors like to start at the beginning, so go through conversations with sensors in a linear, sequential order: First A happened, then B happened, then C happened, all the way down to Z. Sensors are usually straightforward and use facts and details to back up what they are saying. Sensors are literal, specific, and precise. Pay close attention as an elicitor: sensors will lay everything out clearly for you in a very organized fashion. When they're asked for direction, they will give step-by-step linear instructions and practical applications. Sensors state topics clearly, so prepare facts and examples ahead of time. Draw on the past using real experiences when communicating with sensors. Use facts and evidence to back up your claims. Be straightforward. Speak in a linear, sequential order. Respect their experiences and be patient as they work their way to the point they are trying to make. Don't skip over important details or steps. Offer examples that relate to real life. Pique their curiosity by talking about tangible experiences or practical applications: what you can do or how things can be used. Try to use concrete language if possible. Don't go off on tangents. Sensors like to discuss one topic at a time.

Suggested Elicitation Techniques

Presumptive statement
Bracketing
Quotation of reported facts
Naïveté
Status manipulation

BASIC COMMUNICATION TACTICS TO UTILIZE IN ELICITING THE TRUTH FROM INTUITIVES

Communicating with Intuitives

Spark their curiosity with ideas and theories, engage their imagination, and focus on future possibilities and ideas rather than the present moment. A lot of concrete data or detail will bore intuitives or overwhelm them. Try to focus on the "big picture." Don't try to convince them of anything, because it's "the way it's always been done" or it's "traditional." Intuitives use a lot of analogies, metaphors, and euphemisms as descriptors rather than real-life examples. Intuitives enjoy playing play devil's advocate. Intuitives like to talk about possibilities, what could happen, what will happen, and the meaning behind things. Intuitives like new and novel ideas. Intuitives like to brainstorm options, but don't overwhelm them with details.

Suggested Elicitation Techniques

Presumptive statement (presenting a true or false statement)

Feigned or real disbelief
Curiosity
Empathetic exclamations
Be a skeptic

THINKING AND FEELING

Ask yourself, *How do I make decisions?* If you prefer to make decisions by objectively evaluating the facts, analyzing the pros and cons, and examining the logical consequences of your choices or actions, then your preference is for thinking. If you prefer to make decisions by seeking input from other people, making sure everyone involved in the decision is heard, and seek to create harmony, then your preference is for feeling.

A Deeper Dive

People who prefer thinking are objective, analytical, weigh the pros and cons, and analyze situations logically and impersonally. Thinkers have a more difficult time interacting with other people because they think it is more important to tell the truth even if the truth offends other people. Thinkers try to persuade people using logical arguments often ignoring other people's emotions and feelings. Thinkers take pride in their ability to step back and make fair and objective decisions. Thinkers apply one standard and think the standard should be applied to all people regardless of the consequences. Thinkers are often surprised that something they said offended another person. Thinkers typically use the word "think" when they speak.

People who prefer feeling are people pleasers. Feelers are more attentive to other people because feelers want to be liked by everybody. Feelers will go to great lengths to help others, often forgetting about their own needs. Feelers often interject themselves into other people's problems and make the problems their own. Feelers have tender egos and are hurt more easily and more often. Feelers are comfortable telling white lies to avoid the possibility of hurting another person. Feelers tend to avoid unpleasant topics or, when obligated to respond, will use misdirection and half-truths to avoid embarrassing themselves or others. Feelers are more concerned with harmony and mercy and will seek extenuating circumstances to circumvent rules and standards. Feelers typically use the word "feel" when they speak.

BASIC COMMUNICATION TACTICS TO UTILIZE IN ELICITING THE TRUTH FROM THINKERS

Communicating with Thinkers

If your elicitation target prefers thinking, talk to them in analytical terms, keeping in mind their need for rules and routines. Thinkers analyze the pros and cons before making decisions or solving problems. Thinkers tend to see things in black-and-white and identify logical inconsistencies. Thinkers make decisions based on logic and reason, often overlooking emotions and feelings. Thinkers are organized and logical. When eliciting from thinkers, consider the cause and effect, focus on consequences, don't ask how they feel, ask what they think, and appeal to their sense of fairness.

Suggested Elicitation Techniques

Bracketing
Exploiting the instinct to complain
Feigned or real disbelief
Quotation of reported facts
Curiosity

BASIC COMMUNICATION TACTICS TO UTILIZE IN ELICITING THE TRUTH FROM FEELERS

Communicating with Feelers

Feelers are compassionate and have a warm nature. When eliciting from feelers, seek consensus by inviting input and alternate viewpoints before making decisions. Feelers will ignore past solutions and recommendations if the outcome goes against the "greater good." They're also very persuasive. When communicating with feelers, first mention points of agreement, express appreciation for their efforts and contributions, recognize the legitimacy of feelings, and talk about people's concerns. Smile and maintain good eye contact with feelers and be friendly and considerate.

Suggested Elicitation Techniques

Third-party perspective
Empathetic exclamations
Presumptive statement
Naïveté (inexperienced)
Be a skeptic

JUDGING AND PERCEIVING

Ask yourself, *How do you deal with the outer world?* If you prefer to live in a planned, orderly manner, stick to a plan or schedule, and seek to regulate and manage your life, then your preference is for judging. If you prefer to live a flexible, spontaneous life, seeking a variety of experiences, then your preference is for perceiving.

A Deeper Dive

People who prefer judging like organization, structure, and closure. Judgers are rule followers. Judgers like to make plans and stick to the plans and become anxious when things do not go according to the plans. Judgers like to know their place in social and business hierarchies and respect authority. Judgers need to be in control of situations. Judgers often become impatient when things bog down and will often step in and take charge. Judgers respect time and are rarely late for appointments. Judgers meticulously plan out their lives and see time as a means to accomplish their goals. Judgers are precise and rigidly adhere to deadlines. Judgers have a strong work ethic. Judgers need to be constantly productive, they have a place for everything, and everything must be in its place. Judgers seek closure as soon as practical.

People who prefer perceiving are flexible, spontaneous, and like to keep their options open. They have a difficult time making decisions, because they continually seek input. Perceivers often become anxious when they are forced to make a quick decision. They don't like to be hemmed in by rules that restrict their freedom and spontaneity. Perceivers see deadlines as mere guidelines. People with a preference for perceiving like to procrastinate, putting off work until the last minute. They enjoy the process and place less emphasis on the end result of a project or activity. Perceivers are rebels and tend to question authority, but at the same time they do not mind letting other people make decisions. They will do something and then ask for forgiveness later. Perceivers have strong opinions but see things in shades of gray rather than in black-and-white. They are less conscientious about their duties and responsibilities to others.

BASIC COMMUNICATION TACTICS TO UTILIZE IN ELICITING THE TRUTH FROM JUDGERS

Communicating with Judgers

When communicating with judgers, be organized and efficient and don't waste their time. Since judgers make decisions quickly, encourage them to come to conclusions using timelines and specific objectives. Eliciting from judgers requires efficient communication and well-defined terms and conditions. They like structure and expect punctuality. Judgers don't like open-ended discussions and they like to receive information ahead of time. When possible, elicitors should preface their encounter with relevant information before beginning the elicitation portion of the conversation.

Suggested Elicitation Techniques

Presumptive statement
Quid pro quo
Quotation of reported facts

Word echo
Feigned disbelief

BASIC COMMUNICATION TACTICS TO UTILIZE IN ELICITING THE TRUTH FROM PERCEIVERS

Communicating with Perceivers

When communicating with perceivers, expect many questions. Don't force them to make quick decisions. Give perceivers choices and be prepared to give them several options to choose from. Since perceivers are flexible, spontaneous, and are open to unexpected requests, they are less likely to be alerted by more direct inquiries and provide more information in the form of options. Eliciting information from perceivers can be enjoyable, because they are playful and enjoy banter.

Suggested Elicitation Techniques

Feigned or real disbelief
Word echo (repeating the last word spoken)
Curiosity
Status manipulation
Bracketing

SECTION III

PUTTING YOURSELF TO THE TEST

CHAPTER 14

Can You Meet the Counter-Elicitation Challenge?

You learn something valuable from all of the significant events and people, but you never touch your true potential until you challenge yourself to go beyond imposed limitations.

ROY T. BENNETT

At this point in human history, very few people know about elicitation and how it can be used as a truth detector to painlessly gain information from individuals without them realizing what is happening. One reason for this is because the approach is relatively new. Also, very little has been published on the subject. This gives you a definite advantage when you use elicitation. Because so few people know about it, they have not built up defenses to counteract its power. And even if they do learn of the approach, it will still be difficult to overcome, because elicitation is like a stealth fighter, able to breach the natural brain defenses that would normally detect, deflect, and/or defeat the tactic.

This brings me to an interesting question: Now that you

know about elicitation, what it can do, and how it works, does that make you immune to being effectively elicited by someone else?

Well, yes and no. It does give you a better chance of detecting elicitation when you are being targeted, but you still must be very alert—and regularly drill yourself on staying alert—to its potential to "sneak" through your defenses and cause you to reveal truths you might have otherwise left unsaid.

NAME IT AND CLAIM IT

Your best defense against elicitation being used against you is identifying it, giving it a label, and seeing it as a total entity. Imagine back to the early 1980s when doctors were baffled by a serious number of unusual medical problems in young men, oftentimes leading to death. Until the medical community could put a label on this mysterious problem, they were unable to develop a treatment to combat the disease. It was only when the "big picture" became clear, and it was recognized that underlying all these health issues was a new disease, AIDS, that steps could be taken to slow the spread of the affliction, find effective drugs to control it, and shift it from an almost automatic death sentence to a manageable medical condition.

What was true with AIDS is also true with elicitation. Until you can get a handle on the overall process, it will be very difficult for your brain to diagnose its use and its effects. You now have the name of the process and understand what it can do. *Just realizing elicitation exists increases the odds that you will be able to recognize and resist it.* But because it works subtly, based on human nature, you must remain constantly vigilant that you do not fall victim yourself. One way to give you an edge in this area is a strategy developed by my son.

BRYAN'S LOOP

Several years ago I was one of the instructors in a military interrogation training class. The final weeklong exercise tested the skills of the newly minted interrogators. The last exercise was designed to emulate actual field conditions.

To make the scenario as real as possible, role players acted out their scripted parts during mock crimes. If the scenario called for a witness to overhear a conversation in a restaurant, they sat in a booth adjacent to the table in which the suspects were seated. The suspects discussed plans for a terrorist attack. Since the witness overheard the conversation, their reporting would be realistic. Likewise, every role player acted out their part in a realistic setting.

As the scenario developed, the interrogators were required to question suspects in order to obtain additional information to identify the individuals involved in the planned terrorist attack. To make things more challenging, witnesses were instructed to provide information that would lead interrogators to dead ends. These witnesses were referred to as "red herrings."

My son, Bryan, was one of the role players. He was assigned the role of being the leader of the terrorist plot. During his first interrogation, the interrogators determined that Bryan was a red herring and recommended that he be released from custody. The instructor, knowing Bryan was the leader of the plot, cautioned the interrogators that if Bryan were to be released, he would resume his normal life. In doing so, interrogators would have to locate Bryan going about his daily activities and detain him for a second interview. Taking the subtle hint, the interrogators reinterviewed Bryan. After the second interview, they came to the same conclusion.

I later asked Bryan how he was able to evade detection during both interrogations. He described a simple technique that he had developed. First, he made up his mind about the information that he would release. In this instance Bryan assumed the role of a farmer who was stopped at a checkpoint. During an inspection of his pickup truck, bomb-making material was discovered. Bryan was taken into custody to be interrogated. The only information he decided to disclose was that he was a farmer trying to eke out a living for his wife and children.

Bryan decided to answer interrogation questions in three ways: yes plus, no plus, or I don't know plus. The plus was information that Bryan previously had decided to release. For example, if the interrogator asked, "Are you a terrorist?" Bryan answered, "No, I am a farmer."

Simply stated, Bryan answered "Yes," "No," or "I don't know," then told the interrogators what he had had previously decided to disclose.

To further confuse his interrogators, Bryan displayed the nonverbal friend signals that were discussed earlier in the book. At the same time he told his interrogators that he was a farmer in a variety of ways such as "I grow crops," "I raise animals," and "I'm a farmer trying to support my family."

Because Bryan displayed friend signals, he was able to suck his interrogators into a loop they did not know how to break. In fact, during a debriefing, the interrogators did not even realize they had been caught in a loop. I labeled this counter-elicitation technique "Bryan's loop" to give him full credit for discovering this tactic.

Most readers of this book are not going to be subjected to

interrogation, but they will face possible elicitation attempts in business, political, and social environments. Therefore, I modified Bryan's loop to work in these circumstances. The modified version is to answer, "Yes plus," "No plus," or "I don't know plus," and then redirect the conversation back to the person making the inquiry.

I taught this modified Bryan's loop to U.S. embassy officials around the world. These officials found the modified Bryan's loop to be extremely valuable. Embassy personnel often attend formal and informal social functions. At these events, the embassy officials meet with intelligence officers and diplomats from foreign countries who try to elicit sensitive information from their American counterparts. Using Bryan's loop, the U.S. embassy officials only released the information they had earlier programmed themselves to release and put the ball back into their counterparts' court. For example:

FOREIGN DIPLOMAT: I heard that the U.S. is going to deploy additional troops to the Middle East. [Presumptive statement.]

U.S. EMBASSY OFFICIAL: I don't know [chosen from "Yes," "No," or "I don't know"). I work as a public relations officer at the embassy [the "plus" part of the "I don't know"]. With your job, you are in a far better position to know such things. Where did you get your information? [Redirecting the inquiry while flattering his counterpart at the same time.]

One of my former students told me he used Bryan's loop with great results. The student was assigned to conduct an undercover intelligence operation in a hostile country. The student landed at the airport and stood in the customs and immigration line. A few minutes later an immigration official tapped the student on the shoulder and pulled him out of the line. The student's heart raced. He thought he was caught. After a few seconds the student's training kicked in. He remembered the spotlight effect (where people who lie or are trying to hide something believe that everyone around them can detect their deception or intent). The student knew he was undercover but realized the immigration official did not know he was an intelligence officer.

The student then remembered Bryan's loop. His heart rate returned to normal and he was confident his training would protect his cover. He reported that he breezed through the barrage of questions from the immigration official using Bryan's loop and a generous amount of friend signals.

In the end, the immigration official believed the student and released him into the country. The immigration official had no inkling that he had been caught in Bryan's loop. As it turned out, the student had been randomly selected from the customs and immigration line: the customs and immigration official had no idea that the student was on a secret undercover mission. The student later told me that without Bryan's loop he might have gone into the freeze/fight/flight response, breaking his cover. He pointed out, furthermore, that Bryan's loop was simple to remember and execute even under the most stressful conditions. Bryan's loop is an excellent counter-elicitation technique.

BEWARE OF THE "JIGSAW PUZZLE" EFFECT

There's an old saying: "Fool me once, shame on you; fool me twice, shame on me." This bit of folk wisdom has serious implications for you as you take steps not to fall victim to counter-elicitation. Of course, the greatest way to avoid being victimized by an effective elicitation is never to speak. That's not going to happen. What usually happens is that, if you're alert to the possibility of being elicited, you might give away one piece of information before you realize that you are being targeted. If the elicitor tries to get additional information, *then* your counter-elicitation radar should pick up the threat. Thus, the fool-me-once, fool-me-twice adage takes on special significance.

Some elicitors are aware that prolonged elicitations can set off alarm bells in people who know and practice the approach. Therefore they don't try to find out everything they need to know at once. They are confident they can probably elicit one piece of critical information (the fool-me-once approach) but not two or more (the fool-me-twice result). So how do they get to the truth? By bits and pieces, seeking information from one individual on multiple occasions or multiple individuals on one occasion. Then, when enough pieces of information have been procured, they are pieced together like a jigsaw puzzle until a complete picture of what they need to see is pieced together.

One of the pioneers of the elicitation approach to truth detection is John Nolan. In his book, he presents how this "jigsaw puzzle" elicitation approach can work to gather critical information in the workplace:

> If I'm working on an intelligence project for a government contractor who is competing for a multimillion-dollar Federal project, you'll want to learn as much as possible about your opposition, so you can make a better estimate of what their bid is likely to be, based on their various operating expenses. One such expense involves their billing rate structure. That

is, what is the multiplier for Overhead and General and Administrative costs? This involves learning the Company's *overhead rate.*

Can you ask any one person for that information and have a reasonable expectation that they'll provide it? Not in this lifetime. Most people have no idea whatsoever what their firm's overhead rate is. And, even if they did, they would realize it is some of the most valuable proprietary information the company has. Those who do know it would sooner have their hands and heads chopped off before revealing it.

So how do we obtain such fine-tuned numbers? Largely from people who know many small things. Small things that they don't think are important. Naturally, we get some data from government agencies through the Freedom of Information Act. Yet, there are some 160 variables that go into calculating rates, many of which are not available through source documents; variables that can only come from source people. Information on benefits, insurance, building and facilities cost, company paid vacation, equipment costs, number of people involved in the administration of a company, et cetera. People provide this kind of current and necessary data.

For example, an employee responds well to you as a sympathetic inquirer about her insurance package. "It was wonderful five years ago when I got medical, dental, optical for myself, my husband, and my children without any contributions. Now, I'm paying $62.50 per pay period for the most basic coverage." Does that one variable exert a significant downward influence on the firm's overhead structure? You bet. Does the employee consider this to be especially sensitive or proprietary information that she needs to protect? Certainly not. And so, this elicited information becomes one piece of the puzzle after we've confirmed this a few other ways, compared it to prevailing costs of insurance in that marketplace, and find it to be accurate.

Another employee complains to one of the investigators that while he used to get ten days of paid vacation that came out of overhead for the Christmas Season, the bean counters have taken over. The new policy is only two days of company paid vacation. Does that have a significant, and downward, impact on the overhead rate? Absolutely. Again, the employee doesn't appreciate the value of that one bit of information. But, as it is added to the mix of information that you're collecting and verifying from multiple other sources, you can ultimately reach a highly accurate number for the company's overhead rate. Individual pieces, by themselves, aren't that important. Sources rarely recognize the intelligence process at work. That is, they hardly ever see the relationship between the pieces and the puzzle that they are helping to put together.

HACKED BY BITS AND PIECES

Have you ever wondered how major companies end up getting their computers hacked? One would think that these multimillion-dollar organizations would have the security in place to stop such practices. To show you how it can be done, illustrate how bits and pieces of information carefully collected can add up to a major problem, and give you advance warning so you don't fall prey to this kind of illegal manipulation, here is a scenario where one person uses rapport building, elicitation, and some clever maneuvers to hack into a company's computer system. The authors thank Nathan House, a cybersecurity expert, for supplying us with this eye-opening example of corporate espionage.

Background: "Nathan," the would-be hacker, is going to make a series of calls on his mobile phone to the organization he has targeted. His goal is to get access into the company computers so he will have to extract information otherwise unavailable to him. Below, he explains step by step what he does and why he does it (what information he is trying to gain).

Call #1: To the Company's Main Switchboard

> NATHAN: Hi, I'm having a problem with my desk phone. Can you put me through to someone who may be able to sort this out for me?
>
> RECEPTIONIST: Connecting you.
>
> PHONE SERVICES: Hi.
>
> NATHAN: Hi. I'm having a problem with my desk phone. Sorry, I'm new there. Is here any way I can find out who is calling me when they call my desk phone? Is there a caller ID?
>
> PHONE SERVICES: Not really, because we use hot desks here. [A hot desk is a desk shared by more than one person, sometimes several people over three separate shifts.] Because people usually use their mobile phones, the caller ID isn't often related to a name. Is this a problem for you?
>
> NATHAN: No, it's fine now. I understand. Thanks. Bye.

I now know that the company uses hot desks and that phone caller ID is not always expected. Therefore it is not an issue if I call from outside the company. If it was expected, then I could work around it anyway.

Call #2: To the Company's Main Switchboard

NATHAN: Hi, could you put me through to building security?

RECEPTIONIST: Okay.

BUILDING SECURITY: Hello, how can I help you?

NATHAN: Hi, I don't know if you will be interested, but I found an access card outside the building which I think someone must have dropped.

BUILDING SECURITY: Just return it to us. We are in Building 3.

NATHAN: Okay, no problem. May I ask who I'm speaking to?

BUILDING SECURITY: My name's Eric Wood. If I'm not here, give it to Neil.

NATHAN: Okay, that's great. I will do. Are you the head of building security?

BUILDING SECURITY: It's actually called Facilities Security, and the head is Peter Reed.

NATHAN: Okay, thanks a lot. Bye.

This exchange told me the names of a few people in Security, the correct name of the department and the head of security, and that they are the ones who deal with physical access cards.

Call #3: To the Company's Main Switchboard

> **NATHAN:** Hi, I'm calling from the Agency Group and I wonder if you could help me. I had a meeting about a month ago with some of your HR people, but unfortunately my computer crashed and I have totally lost their names.
>
> **RECEPTIONIST:** Sure, no problem. Let me look up that department. Have you any idea at all of their names?
>
> **NATHAN:** I know that one of them was the head of HR. There were a number of people in the meeting, though.
>
> **RECEPTIONIST:** [Pause.] Okay, here we are. Head of HR is Mary Killmister. XXX-XXXX."
>
> **NATHAN:** Yes, that rings a bell. What are the other names in HR?"
>
> **RECEPTIONIST:** In HR, Jane Ross, Emma Jones . . .
>
> **NATHAN:** Yes, definitely Jane and Emma. Could I have their numbers, please?"
>
> **RECEPTIONIST:** Sure. Jane Ross is XXX-XXXX and Emma Jones is XXX-XXXX. Would you like me to put you through to any of them?
>
> **NATHAN:** Yes. Could you put me through to Emma, please?

I now know the names of the three people in HR, including the head.

Call #4: Call to the Company's Human Resources Department

HUMAN RESOURCES: Hello. Emma Jones.

NATHAN: Hi, Emma. This is Eric from Facilities Security in Building 3. I wonder if you can help me. We have had a problem here with the access card database computer. It crashed last night, and some of the data for the new employees got lost. Do you know who would be able to tell us who the new employees were over the last two weeks, as their access cards will have stopped working? We need to contact them and let them know ASAP.

EMMA: I can help you with this. I'll look up the names and email them to you if that's okay. For the last two weeks, did you say?

NATHAN: For the last two weeks, yes. That's great, thanks, but would it be possible to fax it, as we share one computer for email and that was affected by the computer crash too?

EMMA: Yes, okay. What is your fax number? Oh, and what's your name again?

NATHAN: Mark it to the attention of Eric. I'll have to find out the fax number for you and call you back.

EMMA: Okay.

NATHAN: Do you know how long it will take to find out the information?

EMMA: It shouldn't take me more than thirty minutes.

NATHAN: Will you be able to start working on it straightaway? It's quite urgent.

EMMA: I have a few things to do this morning, but I should have the names this afternoon.

NATHAN: That's great, Emma. Thanks. When you're done, would you be able to call me straightaway so I can start reactivating their cards?

EMMA: Yes, sure. What is your number?

NATHAN: I'll give you my mobile number. That way you're guaranteed to get me. XXX-XXX-XXXX.

EMMA: Okay, sure. I'll call you when I have the list.

NATHAN: Excellent. Thanks. Really appreciate this.

Call #5: To the Company's Main Switchboard

NATHAN: Hello. Could you put me through to IT Support?

RECEPTIONIST: Connecting you . . . [Long wait in the queue.]

IT SUPPORT: Hello, can I have your LS number or your case reference?

NATHAN: I've just got a quick question. Is that okay?

IT SUPPORT: What is it?

NATHAN: A guy from Reuters is trying to send me a presentation and is asking me what the maximum size is for attachments.

IT SUPPORT: It's 5 megabytes, sir.

NATHAN: That's great, thanks. Oh, one more thing. He said it's an .exe file and sometimes those get blocked or something.

IT SUPPORT: He won't be able to send an executable file, as the virus scanners will stop it. Why does it need to be an .exe file?

NATHAN: I don't know. How can he send it to me, then? Could he zip it or something?

IT SUPPORT: Zip files are allowed, sir.

NATHAN: Okay. Oh, one more thing: I can't seem to see my Norton AntiVirus icon in my system tray. The last place I worked, there was a little icon.

IT SUPPORT: We run McAfee here. It's just a different icon—the blue one.

NATHAN: That explains it, then. Thanks. Bye.

I now know that to send an executable via email, it will have to be zipped first and less than 5 MB. I also know that they are using McAfee antivirus.

Call #6: A Few Hours Later, a Call from Emma in Human Resources

EMMA: Hi, is this Eric?

NATHAN: Yes, hi.

EMMA: I have the new employees list for you. Do you want me to fax it?

NATHAN: Yes, please. That would be great. How many are there?

EMMA: About ten people.

NATHAN: I'm not sure the fax is working properly here. Could you possibly read them out to me? I think it will be quicker.

EMMA: Okay. Do you have a pen?

NATHAN: Yes, go ahead.

EMMA: Sarah Jones, Sales. Manager is Roger Weaks . . .
[Reads off the rest of the list.]

NATHAN: Okay, thanks. You have been a real help. Bye.

I now have a list of the new employees over the last two weeks. I also have the departments they belong to and their managers' names. New employees are many times more susceptible to social engineering (influence or control by an outside source) than long-term employees.

Call #7: To the Company's Main Switchboard

NATHAN: Hi, I'm trying to email Sarah Jones but am not sure what the format of your email addresses are. Do you know?

RECEPTIONIST: Yes. It would be sarah.jones@targetcompany .com.

NATHAN: Thanks.

Social Engineering Email

Minutes later, a spoofed email [email message with a forged sender address] is sent.

From: itsecurity@targetcompany.com
To: sarah.jones@targetcompany.com
Subject: IT Security

Sarah,

As a new employee with the company, you will need to be made aware of the company's IT security policies and procedures and, specifically, the employee's "Acceptable Use Policy."

The purpose of this policy is to outline the acceptable use of computer equipment at [target company]. These rules are in place to protect the employee and [target company]. Inappropriate use exposes risks, including virus attacks, compromise of network systems and services, and legal issues.

This policy applies to employees, contractors, consultants, temporaries, and other workers at [target company], including all personnel affiliated with third parties. This policy applies to all equipment that is owned or leased by [target company].

Someone will contact you shortly to discuss this with you.

Regards,
IT Security

Call #8: A Couple of Hours Later, a Call to the Company's Main Switchboard

NATHAN: Hi. Could you put me through to Sarah Jones, please?

RECEPTIONIST: Connecting you.

SARAH: Hello, Sales. How can I help you?

NATHAN: Hi, Sarah. I'm calling from IT Security to brief you on IT security best practices. You should have gotten an email about it.

SARAH: Yes, I got an email about it today.

NATHAN: Okay, excellent. It's just standard procedure for all new employees and only takes about five minutes.

How are you finding things here? Everybody being helpful?

SARAH: Yes, thanks. It's been great. It's a bit daunting starting somewhere new, though.

NATHAN: Yes, and it's always difficult to remember everyone's name. Has Roger introduced you around? [The small talk is designed to build rapport interspersed with more trust building.] Emma Jones is very nice in HR if you need any help with that side of things.

SARAH: Yes, Emma did my HR interview for the job.

NATHAN: Well, I better run through the security presentation with you. Do you have your email open? I'll send you the security presentation now and I can talk you through it.

SARAH: Okay, I see the email.

NATHAN: Okay, just double click on the Security Presentation.zip attachment.

SARAH: Okay . . .

The executable that she ran is, in fact, a cleverly packaged series of scripts and tools created by our wrapper program including within it the RAT (remote access Trojan malware program used to gain control of a computer), a rootkit (allows access to a computer while hiding its existence), a keylogger (keeps track of keystrokes on the computer keyboard), and anything else I may want to add.

When Sarah clicks on the file, the presentation immediately starts. This is just a series of PowerPoint slides telling her not to run executables that she is sent, etc., and other good security practices.

The presentation is branded with all the company logos that were conveniently copied from their public web server, just to add a little more trust. A few seconds later, as she is being taken through the presentation, scripts within the package start to try to disable McAfee and any other PC security that may be found that may help protect the user. Then the rootkit installs itself, hiding all future actions from the operating system or anybody doing a forensic investigation. Next the RAT is hidden and installed. The RAT is made to start every time the machine reboots, and these actions are all rootkitted and hidden. The RAT then looks up any proxy settings and other useful information and tries to make its way out of the network and onto the Internet, ready to get its commands from its master. Obviously, all processes and TCP (Transmission Control Protocol) connections are hidden, and even running things like netstat (network statistics) and task manager (procedures that can be used to detect unsanctioned computer manipulation) will not reveal them.

The RAT connects to the master. I now own the PC and it's time to start looking around and really start hacking! Job done.

• • •

I hope the step-by-step calculated takeover of the target company's computer system gives you pause when it comes to recognizing how (1) bits and pieces of seemingly harmless and easy-to-get information can be used for sinister purposes; (2) by building rapport and trust with a person, it makes them more likely to become unknowing co-conspirators in a devious undertaking; and (3) you need to be constantly alert not to give out information without carefully considering the authenticity of the source requesting it.

A FINAL THOUGHT

Falling victim to an elicitation is to be expected. If it didn't work, there would be no reason to write this book. The advantage you, the reader, have at this point is that you understand what elicitation is and how it works. Only a very few people, primarily in law enforcement and government intelligence services, know about the technique. That makes it *far* easier to identify should someone choose to target you for truthful information.

Whenever someone involves you in conversation, don't go into "automatic response" mode! Think about any possible hidden motive the person talking to you might have as the dialogue unfolds. Be cautious about giving up information, particularly the kinds of data that could be used in identity theft or corporate espionage, and remember that the one piece of information you give up might not seem significant, but, combined with other pieces, it just might be the critical item that brings the jigsaw puzzle together. Finally, if you suspect you are being targeted for elicitation, activate Bryan's loop. That should stymie any attempts to extract critical information by the person speaking with you.

CHAPTER 15

Can You Pass the Elicitation Exam?

TEST #1: WHERE'S WALDO?

Arthur Conan Doyle in his book *The Sign of the Four* illustrates the masterful use of elicitation techniques through his famous detective Sherlock Holmes. In this portion of the story, Sherlock and a dog named Toby have chased their suspect to the end of a small wooden pier. Toby stopped and stared out over the cold, dark water. Sherlock's only hope to find his quarry was to see if he had rented a boat from a nearby boathouse. To avoid raising the suspicions of the owner's wife, Sherlock used elicitation instead of direct questioning to obtain the information he sought.

DIRECTIONS

Below is the conversation that took place between Sherlock and the wife of the man who owned the boathouse. Each sentence of the conversation is numbered. See if you can spot where Sherlock used an elicitation technique and then name it. If you don't want to write your answer in the book, use a scratch piece of paper and place the number of the sentence where the elicitation takes place, along with the name of the elicitation technique, on your answer sheet. Do this without looking back in the book to find the correct answer (although you can do this *after* you have taken the test).

Here is a list of the possible elicitation techniques Sherlock could have employed: (1) presumptive statement, (2) storytelling, (3) third-party perspective, (4) bracketing, (5) naïveté, (6) curiosity, (7) status manipulation, (8) empathetic statement, (9) quotation of reported facts, (10) cognitive dissonance, (11) quid pro quo, (12) being a skeptic, (13) feigned disbelief, (14) word echo, (15) hanging chad, and (16) erroneous misattribution.

Here is a hint to get you started: Sherlock Holmes used *eight* elicitation techniques (not necessarily all different) in his short conversation with the boathouse owner's wife. Good luck! There is no time limit for this exam; take as long as you wish to complete your work.

1. "We are out of luck," said Holmes. "They have taken to a boat here."
2. Several small punts and skiffs were lying about in the water and on the edge of the
3. wharf. We took Toby round to each in turn, but, though he sniffed earnestly, he
4. made no sign.
5. Close to the rude landing-stage was a small brick house, with a wooden placard
6. slung out through the second window. "Mordecai Smith" was printed across it in
7. large letters, and, underneath, "Boats to hire by the hour or day." A second
8. inscription above the door informed us that a steam-launch was kept—a statement
9. which was confirmed by a great pike of coke upon the jetty. Sherlock Holmes
10. looked slowly round, and his face assumed an ominous expression.
11. "This looks bad," said he. "These fellows are sharper than I expected. They

12. seem to have covered their tracks. There has, I fear, been preconcerted management
13. here."
14. He was approaching the door of the house, when it opened, and a little, curly
15. headed lad of six came running out, followed by a stoutish, red-faced woman with
16. a large sponge in her hand.
17. "You come back and be washed, Jack," she shouted. "Come back, you young
18. imp, for if your father comes home and finds you like that, he'll let us hear of it."
19. "Dear little chap!" said Holmes strategically. "What a rosy-cheeked young
20. rascal! Now, Jack, is there anything you would like?"
21. The youth pondered for a moment. "I'd like a shillin'," said he.
22. "Nothing you would like better?"
23. "I'd like two shillin' better," the prodigy answered after some thought.
24. "Here you are, then! Catch! A fine child, Mrs. Smith!"
25. "Lor' bless you, sir, he is that, and forward. He gets a'most too much for me
26. to manage, 'specially when my man is away days at a time."
27. "Away, is he?" said Holmes in a disappointed voice. "I am sorry for that, for I
28. wanted to speak to Mr. Smith." [Holmes pivoted toward the objective.]
29. "He's been away since yesterday mornin', sir, and, truth to tell, I am beginnin'
30. to feel frightened about him. But if it was about a boat, sir, maybe I could serve
31. as well."
32. "I wanted to hire his steam-launch."
33. "Why, bless you, sir, it is in the steam-launch that he has gone. That's what
34. puzzles me; for I know there ain't more coals in her than would take her to about
35. Woolwich and back. If he's been away in the barge, I'd ha' thought nothin'; for
36. many a time a job has taken him as far as Gravesend, and then if there was much
37. doin' there he might ha' stayed over. But what good is a steam-launch without coal?"
38. "He might have bought some at a wharf down the river."
39. "He might, sir, but it weren't his way. Many a time I've heard him call out at
40. the prices they charge for a few odd bags. Besides, I don't like that wooden-legged
41. man, wi' his ugly face and outlandish talk. What did he want always knockin'
42. about here for?"

43. "Ah, a wooden-legged man?" said Holmes with bland surprise.

44. "Yes, sir, a brown, monkey-faced chap that's called more'n once for my old

45. man. It was him that roused him up yesternight, and, what's more, my man knew

46. he was comin', for he had steam up in the launch. I tell you straight, sir, I don't

47. feel easy in my mind about it."

48. "But, my dear Mrs. Smith," said Holmes, shrugging his shoulders, "you are

49. frightening yourself about nothing. How could you possibly tell that it was the

50. wooden-legged man who came in the night? I don't quite understand how you can

51. be so sure."

52. "His voice, sir. I knew his voice, which is kind o' thick and foggy. He tapped

53. at the winder—about three it would be. 'Show a leg, Matey,' says he: 'time to turn

54. out guard.' My old man woke up Jim—that's my eldest—and away they went, without

55. so much as a word to me. I could hear the wooden leg clackin' on the stones."

56. "And was this wooden-legged man alone?"

57. "Couldn't say, I am sure, sir. I didn't hear no one else."

58. "I am sorry, Mrs. Smith, for I wanted a steam-launch, and I have heard good

59. reports of the— Let me see, what is her name?"

60. "The *Aurora*, sir."

61. "Ah! She's not that old green launch with a yellow line, very broad in the beam?"

62. "No, indeed. She's as trim a little thing as any on the river. She's been fresh

63. painted—black, with two red streaks."

64. "Thanks. I hope that you will hear soon from Mr. Smith. I am going down the

65. river; and if I should see anything of the *Aurora* I shall let him know that you are

66. uneasy. A black funnel, you say?"

67. "No, sir; black with a white band."

68. "Ah, of course. It was the sides which were black. Good-morning, Mrs. Smith.—

69. There is a boatman here with a wherry, Watson. We shall take it and cross the

70. river."

71. "The main thing with people of that sort," said Holmes, as we sat in the sheets

72. of the wherry, "is never to let them think that their information can be of slightest

73. importance to you. If you do, they will instantly shut up like an oyster. If you listen
74. to them under protest, as it were, you are very likely to get what you want."

End of Test
The answers can be found at the end of this chapter.

TEST #2: HOW LOW CAN YOU GO?

What follows is a conversation between myself and a car salesperson I met at a trade show. We engaged in some small talk
and parted. Coincidentally, I saw him later that evening at a
restaurant where I had dinner. The salesperson invited me to join
him for an after-dinner drink at the hotel bar. I was shopping
around to buy a new car at the time, but I didn't reveal this to the
salesperson. I wanted to learn some truthful information to gain
an advantage when I negotiated the price, I wanted to ask the
salesperson direct questions, but I knew an interrogation-type
conversation would put him off. I decided to use elicitation to
get the information I needed.

I knew elicitation would take longer than direct questioning
to find out what I wanted to know, but I also knew that information would probably be more truthful and detailed using elicitation as opposed to direct questioning. After spending about
fifteen to twenty minutes building rapport, I began the elicitation process. The conversation between us is provided below.

DIRECTIONS

Read through the conversation between myself and the salesperson. Each time I speak, my comments will be numbered consecutively from 1 to 18. Your task is to indicate which of my comments utilized an elicitation technique and to name the technique from the following sixteen: (1) presumptive statement, (2) storytelling, (3) third-party perspective, (4) bracketing, (5) naïveté, (6) curiosity, (7) status manipulation, (8) empathetic statement, (9) quotation of reported facts, (10) cognitive dissonance, (11) quid pro quo, (12) being a skeptic, (13) feigned disbelief, (14) word echo, (15) hanging chad, and (16) erroneous misattribution.

HINT: SOME STATEMENTS USE TWO ELICITATION TECHNIQUES AT ONCE. IN SUCH CASES, IF YOU JOT DOWN EITHER ONE OF THEM, CONSIDER THE ANSWER TO BE CORRECT.

Once again, if you don't want to write your answers in the book, use a scratch piece of paper and place the number of the sentence where the elicitation takes place, along with the name of the elicitation technique, on your answer sheet. Do this without looking back in the book to find the correct answer (although you can do this *after* you have taken the test). The answers to this test can be found at the end of the chapter.

One final point before you start the test (which is untimed). What you read represents an actual conversation. Thus, if you're thinking of purchasing an automobile, what you learn while taking the exam should be of financial benefit to you when you enter your dealership of choice.

1. **Me:** Selling cars must be a tough way to make a living.

   Salesperson: It's not so bad once you figure out how things work.

2. **Me:** Sounds like you know all the tricks of the trade.

   Salesperson: I know a few tricks. You have to in order to survive.

3. **Me:** Well, with the high markup on new cars, you only have to sell a few cars a week to earn a living.

   Salesperson: A few cars a day is more like it.

4. **Me:** Wow, that's a lot of cars.

   Salesperson: It's not how many cars you sell. It's the profit you make on each sale.

5. **Me:** So there's a lot of wiggle room on the price.

   Salesperson: The only number that counts is the price the dealership paid for the car. No salesperson will show you that invoice.

6. **Me:** So are you telling me there's more than one invoice?

   Salesperson: Most car buyers think the factory invoice is the lowest price a dealer will sell a car for. That's not true. I sell hundreds of cars under factory invoice. Here's how it works. There's the MSRP [manufacturer's suggested retail price]—this is the price the manufacturer sets for a car—and then there's the factory invoice. The factory invoice is supposed to be the price the dealer paid to get the car on the lot. The difference between the factory invoice and the MSRP represents the profit the dealer makes. This is just an illusion.

7. **Me:** An illusion.

   Salesperson: Yeah. Dealers get a lot of hidden perks. Let me give you an example of how a typical sales exchange goes. I tell the buyer, "Look at the factory invoice price. We're only making a few hundred dollars on the car if we sell the car at the price you want to pay. You're getting almost fifteen hundred dollars off the MSRP." The buyer typically replies, "Oh, so, there's nothing more you can really do with the price." My answer is "Exactly. You know you're getting a good deal on this car, and we're making a few dollars on the deal." The buyer walks away thinking they got a terrific deal. Not so. What the buyer doesn't know is that the dealer gets a holdback.

8. **Me:** A holdback.

   Salesperson: Yeah. The manufacturer created the holdback to help dealers offset administrative costs. The holdback artificially increases the dealership's cost on paper. The typical holdback is between 1 percent and 3 percent. That means a 3 percent holdback on a $38,000 vehicle is $1,140. On top of the difference between the factory invoice and the MSRP, the dealership makes an additional $1,140.

9. **Me:** Wow, that's unbelievable.

   Salesperson: That's only the beginning. Dealerships get dealer incentives to sell specific models of cars or to sell cars to make room for new models. Dealer incentives can be $2,000 or more. The dealership doesn't always tell the buyer about incentives translating into substantial profits for the dealership. If dealerships meet certain sales quotas, they might also get additional incentives on every car they sell over their quota. A dealership will typically negotiate the holdback or dealer incentives to motivate the buyer. On top of that, dealerships charge dealership fees to get the car showroom ready. That dealer fee can range from $500 to $1,000. The dealer fees, manufacturer incentives, and holdback keep the factory invoice artificially high.

10. **Me:** Sounds complicated.

    Salesperson: Let me simplify things for you. The manufacturer charges the same price for identical vehicles to all dealerships. The real invoice you will never see. You can go online and get a good estimate of the actual cost to the dealership, but the real invoice is privileged information. The dealership then creates a factory invoice. The factory invoice includes the holdback, the dealer fee, the destination fee, and other fees. Add in a 2 to 3 percent profit, and that becomes the MSRP. The goal of any car buyer is to buy the car under the factory invoice. Car salespeople will sell cars all day at or slightly above the factory invoice. The profit margin on a car sold at factory invoice is between $2,000 and $4,000. Imagine the profit on a car sold at MRSP. Since all dealerships are charged the same for comparable vehicles, they become competitive by negotiating a price between the real invoice and the MSRP.

This is the secret to buying a new car. Car salespeople are not going to tell you what I just told you. The dealership is out to get as much as they can from car buyers.

11. **Me:** Whoa, you sure know your stuff!

Salesperson: Oh, there's more.

12. **Me:** You've got to be kidding!

Salesperson: Go to the fleet salesperson.

13. **Me:** Fleet salesperson.

Salesperson: Large dealerships have fleet salespeople. They sell multiple vehicles to companies that have a fleet of cars. Fleet salespeople don't work on commission. They work on volume. They get paid by the number of cars they sell, not by the price the buyer paid for each car. Fleet salespeople will negotiate anything above the real invoice to make a sale. They don't care how much the buyer pays for a car. Their goal is to sell as many cars as possible. If you ask for the fleet salespeople, they will be more than happy to sell you a car. Most large-volume dealerships have fleet salespeople. Another advantage of a large dealership is that they are competing for volume discounts from the manufacturer. This gives the buyer more negotiating power and lets the dealership underbid smaller competitors.

14. **Me:** Oh, wow, that's good to know.

Salesperson: Here's another secret to buying a car: Get preapproved using your own source of financing. It's cheaper than financing a car through the dealership. Okay, here's the trick. Ask the salesperson what the charge-back is for financing through the dealership. If a buyer finances a car through the dealership, the dealer receives a 2 to 3 percent incentive. In order to receive the incentive, the buyer must pay on the loan for at least three to four months. If the buyer doesn't pay on the loan for that long, the dealership is charged back the amount of the incentive. In other words, the dealership must repay the incentive. The financing incentive is another negotiating tool to bring to the table. For example, the buyer could say, 'I'll finance through the dealership one month past the charge-back cutoff in exchange for an additional $500 dollars off the sales price of the car." If the dealership agrees, finance the car through the dealership, pay the loan one month past the charge-back deadline, and then pay off the loan with your preapproved financing at a lower interest rate.

15. **Me:** Interesting.

   Salesperson: Dealerships take delivery of cars on consignment. In other words, they don't have to pay for a car unless the car is sold. If the dealership doesn't sell the car within ninety days, they must pay interest on the price of the car. Look for a car that's been on the lot for a long time, and the dealership will likely sell it at a lower price to avoid paying the interest.

16. **Me:** Finding out how long a car has been on the lot must be difficult.

   Salesperson: It's easy. Just look on the edge of the driver's-side door. The date the car was manufactured is stamped on the sticker. Add four or five weeks, and that gives you a good idea when the car arrived on the lot. Other good times to buy a new car are at the end of the month and at the end of the year. This is typically when sales quotas are calculated. If the salesperson or the dealership is close to meeting a sales quota, the price of the car will be more flexible. They just want to meet the sales quota to be eligible for manufacturer incentives for the following sales period.

17. **Me:** Yeah, I read about that on the Internet.

   Salesperson: I'll leave you with this. If you don't do your homework, you will be at a big disadvantage when buying a new car. The dealership knows exactly what they paid for every car on their lot. You don't. Your job is to get on the Internet and find out as much as you can about the car you want to buy. Identify the markups, subtract the markups from the MSRP, then subtract several thousand dollars and make that your starting point in the negotiations.

18. **Me:** I'm glad I talked to you before I bought a car.

End of Test
Do NOT turn the page and look at the answers
until you have completed both tests!

A POINT TO PONDER

The car salesperson test you just took demonstrates that the value of elicitation isn't restricted to law enforcement and intelligence services! Anytime you are looking to discover truthful information that will benefit you interpersonally, financially, or career-wise, elicitation is a valuable way to learn what you need to know. In my case, the hour or so I spent eliciting information from the car salesperson saved me thousands of dollars on the next car I purchased. Elicitation created an environment that encouraged the salesperson to tell me the truth about buying a car. And our exchange, besides saving me lots of money, illustrates a vital point about *The Truth Detector*. Elicitation is a conversation with a purpose, rather than an interrogation meant to test for deceit and/or force people to be forthright.

Answers to the Sherlock Holmes Test

Your task was to identify the eight times Sherlock Holmes used elicitation techniques to learn truthful information he sought. You were also asked to name the specific Elicitation Technique being used by Holmes in his elicitation. Here are the answers:

Line 24: Allow people to flatter themselves
Line 38: Presumptive statement
Line 43: Feigned disbelief
Lines 48–51: Feigned disbelief
Lines 58–59: Quotation of reported facts
Line 59: Hanging chad
Line 61: Presumptive statement
Line 66: Presumptive statement

Answers to the "How Low Can You Go?" Test

Your task was to identify the elicitation technique used by Jack during his conversation with the car salesman. Here are the answers based on Jack's responses, which are numbered 1 to 18.

1. Presumptive statement
2. Empathetic statement/status elevation/flattery
3. Presumptive statement
4. Feigned disbelief /status elevation /allow people to flatter themselves
5. Presumptive statement
6. Presumptive statement/feigned disbelief
7. Word echo
8. Word echo
9. Feigned disbelief
10. Empathetic statement
11. Status elevation/allow people to flatter themselves
12. Feigned disbelief
13. Word echo
16. Presumptive statement
17. Quoting a reported source

CHAPTER 16

Your Truth Detector Elicitation Checklist

Congratulations! You are now in possession of the information you need to know to become a fully functional truth detector. Knowledge without action, however, is knowledge wasted. The only way you will become proficient in elicitation is to practice it on a regular basis, learning which techniques work best for you in the various circumstances you will confront in your everyday life. Like any other skill, truth detection is a perishable commodity and must be continuously exercised and updated to remain viable and successful.

In the book, we covered a lot of material and tried to provide you with enough detailed explanations and examples to help make that material practicable and ready to use. Even so, we thought it might be worthwhile to provide you with a final checklist you can refer to when you are first becoming proficient at elicitation. The checklist will help remind you of the steps you need to take to complete a successful elicitation—kind of like the checklist pilots use to make sure they remember everything they need to do to safely takeoff and land their aircraft. It is our belief that, after a period of time, the points on the checklist will be ingrained in your memory and automatically performed, making the need for a checklist obsolete. That is a good thing: once weaned off the list, you can "wing it" on your own, confident that you are doing all the things necessary to maximize your skill as a truth detector.

Of course, it won't ever hurt to glance back at the checklist occasionally . . . just to make sure you haven't fallen into any verbal traps or deviated from optimal strategy in your conversational approach.

In advance of presenting the checklist, let's define, once again, what elicitation is.

Elicitation is the means whereby, through conversation, you can obtain information from a person without that person becoming sensitive to your purpose.

YOUR ELICITATION CHECKLIST

Steps to Take Before Commencing Your Elicitation

1. Determine what you want to achieve with the elicitation. Specifically, what is the information you are seeking?
2. Have some idea of how you plan to bring the conversation around to your subject matter of interest. This refers to the moment or moments when you "pivot" the conversation from small talk to the topic germane to the information you seek.
3. Remember that a good elicitation is painless. The targeted individual will be unaware of what you are

doing. Furthermore, the target will often like you better after the elicitation and even thank you for having the conversation.

4. Don't get spooked by the "spotlight effect," where you *think* that everyone knows *exactly* what you are doing. Again, elicitation, properly conducted, will not arouse suspicion on the part of the targeted person of interest.

5. Recall that elicitation works because it is based on basic human needs and tendencies to act in specific ways to verbal prompts. People *want* to give you the information you seek!

6. Be sure to practice "ego suspension" once the elicitation begins. The elicitation should center around your person of interest, not yourself.

Steps to Take When Commencing Your Elicitation

1. Use rapport-building tactics to make your person of interest more receptive to you both before and during the elicitation. Rapport builds a psychological bridge between people. Individuals are less likely to provide important, truthful information unless rapport is developed. Thus, before you even begin conversing with a person of interest, you will want to establish rapport.

2. As you approach the person of interest, display the "big three friend signals": the eyebrow flash, the head tilt, and the smile.

Steps to Take During the Elicitation

1. Be an active listener throughout the interaction.
2. Begin your conversation with small talk that is *not* related to the subject matter you wish to focus on.
3. During the conversation, when the opportunity presents itself, pivot the focus of the conversation to the subject that contains the information you are seeking to learn.
4. Use one or more of the sixteen elicitation techniques that, based on the circumstances, give you the best chance to acquire the information you seek.
5. When possible, use the "elicitation sandwich" in seeking relevant information.
6. To strengthen rapport, make the person of interest feel good about him- or herself by use of empathetic statements and/or compliments/flattery (if appropriate and/or the opportunity presents itself).

Steps to Take After the Elicitation

1. Once you have acquired the information you sought, make some small talk to pivot away from the topic of conversation that was the focus of your elicitation.
2. Disengage from your person of interest in the same manner as you would after any normal conversation.
3. Process the information you have learned and decide if you need to clarify any of the information you have learned and/or elicit further information from the

person of interest. If so, repeat the elicitation checklist with the person of interest.

4. Continue practicing your elicitation skills whenever possible. Get comfortable with as many of the sixteen elicitation techniques as possible. Remember that being an effective elicitor makes you a more effective truth detector while providing you with a collateral benefit: people will like you better when you use it.

Don't take my word for it! Try the elicitation techniques presented in this book and test your skill to detect the truth before people have a chance to lie.

ACKNOWLEDGMENTS

I would like to express my appreciation to Dave and Lynda Mills of Dave Mills Photography in Lancaster, California, for taking the photographs in this book. Both Dave and Lynda graciously contributed their photographic skills to provide accurate depictions of selected techniques presented in these pages. I would like to thank Andrew Cardone and my daughter, Brooke Schafer, for volunteering their time and talent to serve as models for the photographs in this book. I would like to thank John Nolan, a true master in the art of elicitation, for providing his expert contributions to the book manuscript. His insights and suggestions are greatly appreciated. I would like to thank Michael O'Toole, MD, for providing medical examples where elicitation is suitable in obtaining complete medical histories from patients. A special thanks to Mike Dilley, author and historian, whom I have worked with for many years developing and perfecting the many techniques presented in this book. He also reviewed and edited the manuscript and provided invaluable advice in crafting the final draft.

JACK SCHAFER

I finished my work on *The Truth Detector* on December 31, 2019, marking the end of five decades as a writer. Looking back on my career, I realize I was blessed to work with some of the greatest people in the literary world. What better time than now to recognize them for all they did for me.

To: Kate Fitzgerald, Prentice-Hall editor, who accepted my unsolicited, "over-the-transom" manuscript and published my first novel, *The Last Man Is Out* (1969). Thanks for your support and the risk you took with an unknown author.

To: Paul Reynolds, Malcolm Reiss, Loretta Barrett, and Peter Miller, literary agents extraordinaire, who have represented me with panache and perseverance over the years.

To: Matthew Benjamin and Sean deLone, our two incredibly talented editors, who have done so much to enhance the quality and value of *The Truth Detector*.

To: Each reader who spent his or her precious time reading my books. Thank you! I hope that what you got out of the books justified the time you put into them.

MARVIN KARLINS

APPENDIX A

MBTI Personality Descriptions

More detailed information regarding the MBTI can be found at the Myers & Briggs Foundation website at https://www.myers briggs.org. The following is a brief overview of each of the MBTI personality types.

ENTP (extroversion, intuition, thinking, perceiving): The Visionary

- Processes things intuitively
- First and foremost, wants to understand the world around them
- Sizes up situations quickly, accurately, and with great depth
- Is flexible and adapts well to a variety of tasks
- Is good at the things that most interest them
- Aware of possibilities and are good problem solvers
- Is an idea person
- Gets excited about their ideas, and their enthusiasm is contagious

- Is less interested in developing plans and making decisions
- They find following through on ideas difficult and are apt to not finish what they start
- Is rational and logical at reaching conclusions
- Is a visionary
- Is a fluent conversationalist, has a quick wit, and enjoys verbal sparring
- Enjoys debating and often takes an opposing viewpoint just for the love of debating
- Takes action and makes decisions based on the rule of law
- Isolates themselves from their feelings and from other people
- Under stress, loses the ability to generate ideas and becomes obsessed with minor details
- Values knowledge and seeks higher understanding
- Likes challenges and resolving difficult tasks
- Is creative, clever, curious, and theoretical

ENFP (extroversion, intuition, feeling, perceiving): The Inspirer

- Is warm, enthusiastic, bright, and full of potential
- Lives in a world of possibilities and becomes very passionate and excited about things
- Inspires and motivates others
- Can talk their way in and out of things
- Strives to get the most out of life
- Possesses a broad range of skills and talents
- Is project-oriented
- Has a strong sense of value

- Must do everything according to their strong values
- Is on a continuous quest to achieve inner peace
- Has very good people skills
- Is genuinely warm and interested in people, and places great importance on their interpersonal relationships
- Has a strong need to be liked
- Brings out the best in other people and is well-liked
- Has exceptional ability to intuitively understand other people after a short time
- Feels the details of everyday life are drudgery
- Places little value on detailed maintenance tasks and remains oblivious to these types of concerns
- Gets what they want by means of the gift of gab
- Likes a bit of excitement in their life
- Is basically a happy person
- Works best in situations where they have a lot of flexibility
- Is alert and sensitive, and is constantly scanning their environment
- Often suffers from muscle tension
- Has a strong need to be independent
- Is charming, ingenuous, risk-taking, sensitive, people-oriented

ENFJ (extroversion, intuition, feeling, judging): The Giver

- Is people-focused
- Lives in a world of people possibilities
- Understands and cares about people
- Brings out the best in others

- Is mainly interested in giving love, support, and a good time to other people
- Makes things happen for other people
- Has the ability to make people do what they want them to do
- Tends to be difficult on themselves and thinks dark thoughts when alone
- Avoids being alone
- Fills their life with activities that focus on people
- Focuses on the needs of others and often neglects their own needs
- Is more reserved than other extroverts
- Serves as a catalyst of change in other people
- Tends to feel lonely
- Expresses personal beliefs as long as they are not too personal
- Tends not to reveal their true self
- Is well organized and good at resolving ambiguities
- Exudes self-confidence
- Doesn't like dealing with logic and facts unless connected with people
- Enjoys planning more than achievements
- Has a strong need for close, intimate relationships and expends a great deal of energy maintaining relationships
- Is very loyal and trustworthy once involved in relationships
- Sees growth potential in others

ENTJ (extroversion, intuition, thinking, judging): The Executive

- Is a natural-born leader
- Seeks challenges and wants to be the person to overcome them
- Lives in a world of possibilities
- Has a drive for leadership
- Grasps complexities quickly
- Can absorb large amounts of impersonal information
- Makes quick, decisive decisions
- Takes charge of people
- Is career-focused
- Sees the long term
- Is good at identifying plans to overcome problems, especially in the corporate environment
- Is tireless in their efforts on the job and can visualize where the organization is headed
- Is a natural corporate leader
- Does not allow much room for error
- Dislikes seeing mistakes repeated
- Has no patience for inefficiency
- Is not tuned in to people's feelings
- Has little patience for people who do not see things their way
- Is forceful, intimidating, and overbearing at work, as a parent, and toward a spouse
- Forcefully achieves goals
- Is susceptible to self-aggrandizement
- Is quick to verbalize opinions and decisions

- Believes feelings are a weakness
- Likes to interact with others
- Likes lively, challenging conversations
- Respects people who can argue adroitly
- Is self-confident, with excellent verbal skills
- Desires a congenial and devoted relationship with their spouse
- Focuses on the job and is often physically and emotionally absent while at home

ESFJ (extroversion, sensing, feeling, judging): The Caregiver

- Loves people
- Brings out the best in others
- Is very good at reading people and understanding their point of view
- Has a strong desire to be liked
- Makes people feel good about themselves
- Is warm and energetic
- Takes responsibilities very seriously and is very dependable
- Values security and stability and has a strong focus on the details of life
- Sees before others do what needs to be done and makes sure it gets done
- Needs the approval of others to feel good about themselves
- Is hurt by indifference and doesn't understand unkindness
- Is a very giving person
- Wants to be appreciated for who they are and what they give to others

- Is good at reading others and changing their own manner to be more pleasing to others
- Is not shy about expressing their opinions
- Weighs their values and morals against the world around them, rather than against an internal value system
- Gives the shirt off their back
- Needs to control their environment
- Seeks closure
- Likes to create order and structure
- Likes to control people
- Respects and believes in laws, rules, and authority and believes others should do the same
- Values tradition rather than venturing into uncharted territory
- Tends to blindly follow policies and rules
- Is insecure and focuses on pleasing others
- Tends to be oversensitive and imagines bad intentions when there aren't any

ESFP (extroversion, sensing, feeling, perceiving): The Performer

- Lives in the world of people possibilities
- Likes people and new experiences
- Is lively and fun and likes being the center of attention
- Lives in the here and now
- Enjoys excitement and drama in their life
- Has strong interpersonal skills
- Takes the role of peacemaker
- Is generous and warm

- Is very observant of people
- Is spontaneous and optimistic
- Loves to have fun
- Avoids looking at long-term consequences of their actions
- Believes the entire world is a stage
- Likes being the center of attention
- Constantly puts on a show for others to entertain them and make them happy
- Would like life to be a continuous party in which they play the role of fun-loving host
- Readily accepts others
- Treats everyone as a friend
- Will make strong judgments against people who cross them, forming a deep dislike
- Is very practical but hates routines
- Goes with the flow
- Has the ability to improvise in a variety of situations
- Enjoys hands-on learning rather than reading a book
- Is uncomfortable with theories
- Learns by doing
- Has beautiful possessions and an artfully furnished home
- Has a strong desire to appreciate the finer things in life, such as good food and good wine
- Is a good team player
- Is not likely to cause problems or create a fuss
- Creates a fun environment to get things done
- Likes to feel strongly bonded to other people, animals, and small children
- Appreciates the beauty of nature
- Loves life

- Is liked by everybody
- Lives in the moment

ESTJ (extroversion, sensing, thinking, judging): The Guardian

- Lives in a world of facts and concrete needs
- Lives in the present
- Monitors the environment to make sure everything is running smoothly
- Honors traditions and laws, has a clear set of standards and beliefs, and expects the same from others
- Has no patience for people who do not share their values
- Likes to see quick results for their efforts
- Values competence and efficiency
- Is a take-charge person
- Has a clear vision of the way things should be done
- Naturally steps into leadership roles
- Is self-confident and aggressive
- Is very competent at devising plans with step-by-step procedures
- Can be demanding and critical
- Is straightforward and honest
- Is a model citizen
- Takes commitments seriously
- Can be boisterous and fun at social events
- Is overly detailed oriented
- When under stress, has a hard time expressing their feelings and communicating them to others
- Values social order and security

ESTP (extroversion, sensing, thinking, perceiving): The Doer

- Is an outgoing straight shooter
- Is enthusiastic and excitable
- Is a doer
- Is a blunt, straightforward risk-taker
- Is not afraid to get their hands dirty
- Lives in the here and now
- Places little importance on introspection and theory
- Looks at the facts of the situation, quickly decides what should be done, executes the action, and moves on to the next thing
- Is good at reading facial expressions and stance
- Typically is a couple of steps ahead of the person they are talking to
- Treats rules and laws as merely guidelines
- Doggedly sticks to their strong beliefs
- Places little value on establishment rules
- Has a strong flair for drama and style
- Is fast-moving and fast-talking and likes the finer things in life
- Tends to be a gambler and spendthrift
- Is good at storytelling and improvising
- Makes up things as they go along rather than following a plan
- Loves to have fun
- Is a fun person to be around
- Can hurt other people and not be aware of it
- Doesn't know that their words have an effect on others

- Makes decisions based on fact and logic
- Is impatient with theory
- Is a very good salesperson
- Has an abundance of energy and enthusiasm
- Can sell anyone on any idea

INFJ (introversion, intuition, feeling, judging): The Protector

- Is gentle, caring, artistic, and creative
- Lives in a world of hidden meanings and possibilities
- Rarest of all types (1 percent)
- Likes things orderly and systematic in the outer world
- Constantly defines and redefines priorities in their lives
- Is usually right, and they know it
- Has tremendous faith in their instincts and intuition
- Gets feelings about things
- Is a complex individual
- Doesn't like to share feelings
- Is private and difficult to understand
- Can be secretive
- Avoids hurting people
- Is warm and caring
- Is very sensitive to conflict
- Tends to internalize stress, causing health problems
- Ignores other people's opinions
- Is a perfectionist
- Is rarely at peace with themselves
- Believes in constant growth
- Doesn't believe in compromising ideals

- Is hard-nosed and stubborn
- Is good at dealing with minutiae and very detailed tasks
- Feels life is not easy

ISFJ (introversion, sensing, feeling, judging): The Nurturer

- Takes things in via the five senses in a literal, concrete fashion
- Is kind and warmhearted and sees the best in other people
- Seeks harmony and cooperation and is sensitive to other people's feelings
- Has a rich inner world
- Remembers things that are personally important to other people
- Possesses a large volume of personal information and is usually accurate
- Has an exceptional memory about things that are important to them
- Remembers in great detail conversations that took place years later if the conversations were meaningful to them
- Has a very clear idea of how things should be done
- Values security, kindness, traditions, and laws
- Believes in existing systems because they work
- Is less likely to do things a new way unless they can be convinced that the new way is superior to the traditional way of doing things
- Learns best by doing rather than reading from a book or from a theoretical perspective
- Carries out tasks faithfully to their conclusion

- Has a well-developed sense of space and function and aesthetic appeal, and likely has a beautifully furnished, functional home
- Finds gifts that will be truly appreciated by the recipients
- Is keenly aware of their own feelings and the feelings of others
- Has difficulty expressing their own feelings but can help other people express their feelings
- Feels a strong sense of responsibility and duty
- Takes their responsibilities seriously
- Has a hard time saying no
- Dislikes conflict
- Puts other people's needs above their own
- Has strong feelings of inadequacy and becomes convinced that everything is all wrong or they can't do anything right
- Is warm, generous, and dependable
- Has the ability to keep things running smoothly

INFP (introversion, intuition, feeling, perceiving): The Idealist

- Focuses on making the world a better place
- Has the goal of finding meaning in their life
- Asks: *How can I best serve humanity?*
- Is an idealist and perfectionist
- Drives hard to achieve goals they set for themselves
- Is on a continuous mission to find the truth and meaning underlying things
- Is thoughtful and considerate
- Is a good listener

- Puts people at ease
- Is reserved when expressing their own emotions
- Does not like conflict and goes to great lengths to avoid it
- Considers feelings not who is right or wrong
- Doesn't like feeling bad
- Makes a good mediator
- Is good at solving other people's problems
- Is flexible and laid-back until one of their values is violated
- Is aggressive and fights passionately for their cause
- Seeks causes
- Doesn't like to deal with facts and logic
- Avoids personal analysis
- Problems working in groups
- Is usually a talented writer
- Feels awkward verbally expressing feelings

INTJ (introversion, intuition, thinking, judging): The Scientist

- Lives in a world of ideas and strategic planning
- Values intelligence, knowledge, and competence
- Has high standards and continually strives to fulfill them
- Is very quick to understand new ideas but focuses on applying the ideas
- Is driven to come to conclusions about ideas
- Desires systems and organizations
- Finds it difficult to express internal insights, images, and abstractions
- Is a natural leader but chooses to be in the background until they see a real need to take charge

- Is a supreme strategist
- Spends a lot of time in their own mind and has little interest in other people's thoughts and feelings
- Has trouble with intimacy
- Is quick to express judgment
- Tends to blame misunderstandings on the limitations of other people rather than on their own difficulty expressing themselves
- Tends to dismiss others' input too quickly and becomes generally arrogant and elitist
- Is an ambitious, self-confident, deliberate, long-range thinker
- Values clarity and efficiency
- Often seems aloof and reserved
- Is unlikely to give praise
- Is open to hearing alternative ways of doing things

INTP (introversion, intuition, thinking, perceiving): The Thinker

- Lives in a world of theoretical possibilities
- Thinks in terms of how things can be improved
- Lives inside themselves to analyze difficult problems, identify patterns, and come up with logical solutions
- Seeks clarity in everything
- Is an absentminded professor
- Values knowledge above all else
- Is extremely bright and can be objectively critical in their analysis
- Loves new ideas and becomes very excited over abstractions and theories

- Doesn't like routine tasks
- Appears dreamy and distant
- Does not like to lead or control people
- Is shy when meeting new people
- Tends toward self-aggrandizement and social rebellion
- Is not in tune with people's feelings and has a hard time meeting the emotional needs of others
- May become generally negative and critical
- May become unaware of their environment
- Is not good at paying bills and dressing appropriately
- Insists that ideas must be expressed correctly and succinctly

ISFP (introversion, sensing, feeling, perceiving): The Artist

- Is keenly aware of the way things look, taste, sound, feel, and smell
- Appreciates art
- Is gifted at creating and composing
- Needs to live life according to the way they feel
- Is quiet and reserved
- Is difficult to get to know well
- Holds back their ideas and opinions except from close friends
- Is kind, gentle, and sensitive
- Is an animal lover
- Appreciates nature
- Is original and independent
- Needs to have personal space

- Is action-oriented
- Is a doer
- Is a hands-on learner
- Does not like interpersonal analysis
- Is warm and sympathetic
- Desires to please
- Is service-oriented
- Shows love through actions, not words
- Needs alone time

ISTJ (introversion, sensing, thinking, judging): The Duty Fulfiller

- Is quiet and reserved
- Is interested in security and peaceful living
- Takes in things via the five senses
- Is organized and methodical
- Is very loyal, faithful, and dependable
- Places great importance on honesty and integrity
- Is a good citizen
- Does the right thing for friends, family, and community
- Has an offbeat sense of humor
- Believes in laws and traditions
- Is a rule follower
- Goes "by the book"
- Is extremely dependable and follows through on promises
- Has a hard time saying no
- Often works long hours
- Prefers to work alone
- Likes to be accountable for their actions

- Enjoys being in positions of authority
- Respects facts
- Has a tremendous amount of stored facts
- Once they support an idea, goes to great lengths to support it
- Not tuned in to their own feelings
- Is a perfectionist
- Takes other people for granted
- Is uncomfortable expressing affection
- Is extremely faithful and loyal
- Is traditional and family oriented
- Expresses affection through action not words

ISTP (introversion, sensing, thinking, perceiving): The Mechanic

- Is focused internally
- Deals with things rationally and logically
- Desires to understand the way things work
- Is given to logical analysis
- Has an adventurous spirit
- Is attracted to motorcycles, airplanes, skydiving, and surfing
- Thrives on action
- Is usually fearless
- Is fiercely independent
- Needs space
- Does not believe in or follow rules and regulations
- Does their own thing
- Gets bored quickly

- Believes people should be treated with fairness and equity
- Is loyal and faithful
- Likes to spend time alone
- Is action-oriented
- Likes to be up and about, doing things
- Is adaptable and spontaneous
- Is an effective technical leader
- Focuses on details and practical things
- Can make quick, effective decisions
- Avoids making decisions on personal judgment
- Does not trust their own feelings
- Is good in crisis situations

Glossary of Elicitation Tools

Be a Skeptic. When people are exposed to skepticism, they believe that their statements lack credibility, and they feel the need to add additional information to convince the listener that what they are saying is truthful. Introducing a dash of skepticism into a conversation will encourage the elicitation target to provide more information.

Bracketing. Bracketing sets a range of numbers or dates. The goal of bracketing is to get the elicitation target to provide you with a specific number or date within the bracketing range you present. Bracketing is based on the human need to correct others. Setting a wide bracket encourages people to identify the correct number or date within the bracket.

Cognitive Dissonance. Cognitive dissonance occurs when people are presented with ideas that are in direct opposition to what they think or believe, which in general causes them anxiety. The greater the cognitive dissonance, the more pressure a person feels the need to reduce or eliminate the contradiction and thereby alleviate his/her anxiety and reveal sensitive information.

Curiosity. Curiosity creates an information gap between what people know and what they want to know. Elicitors can intentionally create an information gap predisposing the elicitation target to fill the gap and, in doing so, reveal sensitive information.

Empathetic statements. Empathetic statements identify a person's physical status, emotional situation, or words and using parallel language mirror their physical status, emotional situation, or words back to the speaker. Empathetic statements encourage people to continue speaking. The more people speak, the more information they reveal about themselves and others.

Erroneous misattribution. Erroneous misattribution occurs when the elicitor attributes skills to a person of interest that are not readily associated with that person. An older person is less likely to be adept at social media, just as a small child cannot be expected to solve advanced mathematical problems. Making obviously erroneous attributions prompts elicitation targets to provide reasons why the attributions are incorrect, and, in doing so, they reveal additional information.

Feigned disbelief. Feigned disbelief is an expression of disbelief that puts the targeted subject in a position of defending his or her statement. In doing so, information of value can be revealed.

Hanging chad. The elicitor leaves a thought unfinished, allowing the target to complete the sentence or idea presented by the elicitor, thus providing additional information.

Naïveté. Individuals are predisposed to talk when conversing with someone they perceive is naïve. Playing dumb about a subject encourages the elicitation target to display their expertise to the elicitor and will often reveal sensitive information.

Presumptive statement. A technique whereby the elicitor phrases a piece of information as a simple statement of fact. If the presumptive statement turns out to be correct, the person of interest will affirm the fact and often provide additional information. If the presumptive statement is incorrect, the person of interest will typically provide the correct answer, usually accompanied by a detailed explanation.

Quid pro quo. When offered information first, a person of interest is encouraged to reciprocate by supplying other information.

Quotation of reported facts. Quotation of reported facts means constructing a statement, whether true or false, relevant to the information being elicited, and claiming that you got it from a source such as a newspaper, magazine, blog, TV news, etc. People tend to talk freely if they think the information is in the public domain.

Status manipulation. Status manipulation ascribes either a higher or a lower status to the elicitation target. The target knows that they do not have the talent to live up to the elicitor's expectations or wants to make a convincing argument that they are worthy of a higher status. This disparity induces cognitive dissonance. To reduce the anxiety the cognitive dissonance produces, the elicitation target will tend to reveal more personal and sensitive information during the rationalization process whereby they try to justify the higher status bestowed upon them or provide reasons why they don't merit the status ascribed by the elicitor.

Storytelling. When people hear a story, they often subconsciously insert themselves into it. To be effective, the story should be relevant to your targeted individual's current situation, have a moral, and suggest a course of action that would encourage the person to tell the truth.

Third-party perspective. The elicitor frames information or facts using the third person-perspective, exploiting people's natural tendency to talk about other people. People tend to believe information they hear from a third party, especially when they are being complimented. Hearing things from a third-party perspective gives the illusion that the information must be true because it is coming from a disinterested person. This encourages the target to be more forthcoming about the topic of conversation.

Word echo. Word echo is when the elicitor repeats the last word or two of what the person of interest last said if he or she pauses and needs some encouragement to continue sharing information.

BIBLIOGRAPHY

Briggs-Myers, I., and Myers, P. B. (1980). *Gifts Differing: Understanding Personality Type*. Mountain View, CA: Davis-Black Publishing.

Doyle, A. C. (1930). *The Complete Sherlock Holmes*. Garden City, New York: Doubleday & Company, Inc.

Finkelstein, S. (2017, December 6). "Building Trust in Less Than 10 Minutes." Retrieved from HuffPost: https://www.huffpost.com/entry/building-trust-as-an-anesthesiologist_b_3602250.

Granhag, P. A., Montecinos, C., and Oleszkiewicz, S. (2015). "Eliciting Intelligence from Sources: The First Scientific Test of the Scharff Technique." *Legal and Criminological Psychology* 20, 96–113.

Gueguen, N., Meineri, S., Ruiz, C., and Pascual, A. (2016). "Promising Reciprocity: When Proposing a Favor for a Request Increases Compliance Even if the Favor Is Not Accepted." *Journal of Social Psychology* 156, 498–512.

House, N. (2015, January 8). "Social Engineering Example." Retrieved from *Station X Cyber Security Blog*: https://www.stationx.net/social-engineering-example-2/.

Nolan, J. (1999). *Confidential: Business Secrets; Getting Theirs, Keeping Yours* (2nd ed.). Medford Lakes, NJ: Yardley Chambers.

May, L., and Granhag, P. A. (2016). "Using the Scharff Technique to Elicit Information: How to Effectively Establish the 'Illusion of Knowing It All.'" *European Journal of Psychology Applied to Legal Context* 8, 79–85.

McCorkle, S., and Reese, M. (2018). *Mediation Theory and Practice* (3rd ed.). Los Angeles: Sage Publications.

Minson, J. A., VanEpps, E. M., Yip, J. A., and Schweiter. (2018). "Eliciting the Truth, the Whole Truth, and Nothing but the Truth: The Effect of Question Phrasing on Deception." *Organizational Behavior and Human Decision Processes* 147, 76–93.

Mouton, F., Leened, L., and Venter, H. S. (2016). "Social Engineering Attack Examples, Templates and Scenarios." *Computers and Security* 59, 186–209.

Oleszkiewicz, S, Granhag, P. A., and Kleinman, S. M. (2014). "On Eliciting Intelligence from Human Sources: Contextualizing the Scharff Technique." *Applied Cognitive Psychology* 28, 898–907.

Rogers, C. R. (1961). *On Becoming a Person.* Boston: Houghton Mifflin.

Schafer, J., and Karlins, M. (2015). *The Like Switch.* New York: Simon & Schuster.

Schafer, J. (2010). *Fibs to Facts: A Guide to Effective Communication.* Alexandria, VA: Spiradula Press.

Sklansky, D., and Schoonmaker, A. (2010). *Ducy.* Las Vegas, NV: Two Plus Two Publishing.

Toliver, R. F. (1997). *The Interrogator: The Story of Hanns Joachim Scharff, Master Interrogator of the Luftwaffe.* Atglen, PA: Schiffer Publishing.

Vincent, J., and Threewitt, C. "How Do Those Car Insurance Tracking Devices Work?" *U.S. News & World Report,* February 26, 2018.

Vrij, A., Nunkoosing, K., Paterson, B., Oostervegel, A., and Soukara, S. (2002). "Characteristics of Secrets and the Frequency, Reasons and Effects of Secrets Keeping and Disclosure." *Journal of Community & Applied Social Psychology* 12, 56–70.

Wang, C., and Huang, Y. (2018). "'I Want to Know the Answer! Give Me Fish 'n' Chips!': The Impact of Curiosity on Indulgent Choice." *Journal of Consumer Research* 44, 1052–67.

Wainwright, G. R. (1993). *Teach Yourself Body Language.* London: Hodder Headlines.

Dr. John R. "Jack" Schafer is a retired FBI special agent who is currently employed as an associate professor at Western Illinois University. Dr. Schafer served as behavioral analyst assigned to the FBI's National Security Behavioral Analysis Program, where he developed many of the ideas presented in this book. Dr. Schafer earned a Ph.D. in psychology from Fielding Graduate University in Santa Barbara, California. He owns his own consulting company and lectures and consults in America and abroad. He authored a book titled *Psychological Narrative Analysis: A Professional Method to Detect Deception in Written and Oral Communications.* He also coauthored the text *Advanced Interviewing Techniques: Proven Strategies for Law Enforcement, Military, and Security Personnel.* He has published numerous articles on a wide range of topics, including the psychopathology of hate, ethics in law enforcement, detecting deception, and the universal principles of criminal behavior. Dr. Schafer's most recent coauthored book is the bestseller *The Like Switch: An Ex-FBI Agent's Guide to Influencing, Attracting, and Winning People Over.* Dr. Schafer also writes a blog for psychologytoday.com.

Dr. Marvin Karlins received his Ph.D. from Princeton University in social psychology. He is currently senior full professor of management at the University of South Florida's Muma College of Business. Dr. Karlins consults worldwide and, for twenty years, trained all operational staff at Singapore Airlines. He has published 30 books and more than 150 articles in professional, academic, and popular journals. Several of his coauthored books have become international bestsellers, including *What Every BODY Is Saying: An Ex-FBI Agent's Guide to Speed-Reading People* and *The Like Switch: An Ex-FBI Agent's Guide to Influencing, Attracting, and Winning People Over*. His most recent book, coauthored with Tony March, is *Paying It Backward: How a Childhood of Poverty and Abuse Fueled a Life of Gratitude and Philanthropy*, and was published in 2020. Dr. Karlins is a member of the Authors Guild and the International Federation of Journalists. He also writes a blog for psychologytoday.com. He is married to Edyth, his wife of almost forty-four years, and has one daughter, Amber Nicole.

Ex–FBI Agent JACK SCHAFER

reveals his proven strategies to instantly read people
and influence how they perceive you, so that you
can easily learn how to *turn on the like switch.*

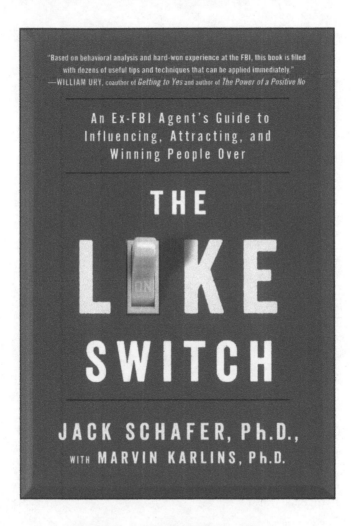

Available wherever books are sold or
at SimonandSchuster.com